Where the Light Finally Lands

Where the Light Finally Lands

The Long Way Home to Yourself

Yeah the Girls 40 Plus

WRITE ANGLES PRESS AND YEAH THE GIRLS 40 PLUS

Published by Write Angles Press in 2025, in collaboration with Yeah the Girls 40 Plus

Write Angles Press ©2025 (Each author in this book owns the copyright for their individual chapter.)

All Rights Reserved. No part of this book may be reproduced by any mechanical, photographic, or electronic processes, or in the form of a phonographic recording. Nor may be stored in a retrieval system, transmitted or otherwise be copied for public or private use other than for 'fair use' - as brief quotations embodied in articles and reviews, without prior written permission of the publisher.

ISBN: (print) 978-1-7642378-2-6

A catalogue record for this book is available from the National Library of Australia

Cover design by Mireille van Yperen (https://www.dtp-hulp.nl/)

Disclaimer

Any opinions expressed in this work are exclusively those of the individual authors and are not necessarily the views held or endorsed by other authors in this publication or Write Angles Press. All of the information and concepts contained within the publication are intended for general information only. The authors and the publisher do not take any responsibility for any choices that any individual or organisation may make with this information in the business, personal, financial, familial or other areas of life. If any individual or organisation does wish to implement the ideas discussed herein, it is recommended that they obtain their own independent advice specific to their circumstances.

Some of the authors in this book have used AI to write their content, based on their own lived experiences. The publisher of this book does not endorse the use of AI.

This book is available in print format.

Contents

Editor's Note	VIII
About Yeah the Girls 40 Plus	IX
Belly of the Beast JJ Collins	1
Childhood Shadows and Their Echoes	5
1. Welcome to the Jungle KM	7
2. The Mirror I Refused to Look Into Melissa Wilkes	19
3. Embracing and Empowering the Sacred Feminine Maria Solano	27
4. From Breakdown to a New Blueprint Anne Barratt	41

5.	How I Lived With ADHD – and How I Would've Lived if I'd Known It Michal Gabriel	55

Loss, Grief and Survival   65

6.	Despair Shaz Cini	67
7.	Life in Moments Sheree Tivendale	83
8.	The Path Back to Pleasure Jo Goddard	91
9.	Twelve Lessons Laurel-lea Jennings	101

Identity Unravelled and Reclaimed   119

10.	Some Days I'm Magnetic, Some Days I'm Just Moisturised Belinda Trisic	121
11.	When 'Normal' Isn't Right: Reclaiming the Wisdom of Your Body in Midlife Sally Pattison	137
12.	Wherever You Go, There You Are – And That's the Point Angela Heise	147
13.	Things I Wish I'd Known When I Was Younger Hannah Babbington	163

Resilience, Renewal and Reinvention   171

14.	The Tassie Move Lee-Anne Kendall	173

15.	Bob O'clock Alice Monaghan	187
16.	Memoir of a Morning: What I Wish I'd Known – a Retrospective JJ Collins	201
17.	Breaking the Silence Jo Jo Sparkle	213
18.	Abused to Ablaze Twee Shaw	223

Purpose, Power and Becoming	**239**

19.	Laying the Foundations of a Dream Life Cecilia Huang	241
20.	Dance Like the World's Not Closing – Even If It Is Adelle Givney	257
21.	The Phoenix Within: Rising from the Ashes Elena Saikova	267
22.	Do Not Follow What Martha Did and You Will Be Very Successful Martha Mok	281

And Now, A Toast JJ Collins	297

Editor's Note

Stories have always been how humans make sense of the world. They remind us that while no two journeys look the same, the need to be heard, seen and understood is universal. This book grew from that belief. *Where the Light Finally Lands – The Long Way Home to Yourself* brings together twenty-two women over the age of forty who said yes to sharing a piece of their lives.

The five sections – from childhood echoes to purpose and becoming – are not neat stages but overlapping truths. You may recognise yourself in one story or in many. You may be reminded of someone you love. You may simply find comfort in knowing you're not alone.

As the editor, I am grateful to each woman who trusted this process and offered her story to the page. And I am grateful to you, the reader, for stepping into these pages with an open heart. May these stories remind you that light does come, even after the darkest nights, and that the journey home to yourself, however long, is always worth taking.

Kellie Nissen

About Yeah the Girls 40 Plus

Yeah The Girls 40 Plus began with one simple belief: women deserve to be celebrated, no matter where they are in life.

What started as a space for connection has grown into a powerful community where women over 40 can feel seen, supported and valued. Here, we share wisdom, laughter, challenges, and triumphs because life after forty is not about fading into the background.

Our purpose is to create a safe, uplifting place where women can connect, learn and thrive together. Whether it's through friendship, business, confidence or personal growth, this group is about reminding every woman that she is not alone and is worthy of celebration.

Martha Mok

Belly of the Beast

JJ Collins

Straight into the belly of the beast she had flown
    Slashing and thrashing
Flesh blood and sweat, all swirling together
The rage and the fury
They weren't going to beat her

It threatened her loved ones
All that she knew
Her very existence
Her soul
Me and you

A dagger she held in each hand, tight as ever
Her forearms, her biceps
The fury, the wrath!

Alone she must face it
The beast come to ruin
No-one can help her
It must come from within

The strength to avenge
The drive to defeat
The knowledge and skill
The hate and the fear

This beast she once knew
Once called it a friend
Though the nurture and solace
Had come to an end

Hacking and gashing seem to go on forever
Her bones and her flesh aches
Her mind starts to tire

The beast starts to weaken
The agony, the moaning
Each tear of its flesh
Is gushing and oozing

The entrails and fluid
She feels like she's drowning
The beast she once knew
Her old friend is now dying

Just for a second
A tiny, short moment
She lamented the torture
The pain she'd inflicted

Despite all the sadness
The depths of despair
It had made her whole
Gave her courage to care

For it was within her
That strength, it had given
Else she wouldn't be her
Incomplete, unforgiven

As she rose from her battle
Exhausted, unscathed
She knew that her fate
Was not sealed, but saved

She had come to realise
The blood was her own
By fighting and striving
She'd opened her wounds

But now she could heal
The air could get in
By facing the beast
It had strengthened …
Not ruined

Childhood Shadows and Their Echoes

Welcome to the Jungle

KM

Spring, and the chilly winter mornings were subsiding. In a wee country hospital, where Mum's midwife – they used to call them Sisters – wanted to get things moving with my birth because she needed to get to the bank!

1983. When the banks closed at 3 pm.

In a rushed fashion, I entered the world soon after all that hustle. A child of '83. The world was filled with paisley shirts, World Series Cricket and episodes of *The Love Boat*. Our family house was almost built. Getting it sealed and ready to live in was of the utmost importance before I came home from hospital, so I'm told.

Not long after I was born, there was major family event – my grandfather had a stroke. I was about six weeks old. He was my mother's father, and so I went from the boob to the bottle while Mum sat with Gramps in his final days. He died six days later. It was a lost connection for me and a deep grief to endure for Mum and the rest of my family. Sometimes I wonder how we'd have gotten along. He was buried in the same place I was born. I still visit every chance I get. The grave went unmarked for many years, so I used to have to remember where he was by counting the rows.

Gramps had been in the Merchant Navy. People who knew him have told me he was a stern man with every angle of hardness you can imagine. That's how men were in his day – hard and stern. He'd divorced my granny years earlier and had some demons with the grog – like many in my family. It's just the way it was. It was in their blood and was the norm. A ship now marks the spot where he's laid to rest. His legacy lives on in my brother and my son – more so as the years have passed. They're long and lanky lads with attitude to boot!

By the time I was about four, my family dynamic had changed. Dad was physically unwell. He'd had terrible asthma most of his life and was breathing in asbestos every day on job sites (not that it was known to be deadly then). He had a fag hanging out of his mouth most of the time and battled to manage the booze.

Mum was … well, it depends on who you ask. She was a working mum with four kids. From my earliest memories, she was just always busy. I only have a handful of recollections where Mum and Dad are still together. I must've been two or three at the time, and once they decided to separate, it felt as though we drifted around for a while. Bits and pieces of momentary joy and terror – all intertwined.

The timeline is sometimes a bit foggy.

What I do remember was when Mum started bringing a new man to the house. I think I was four or five at the time. He'd come to ours, or we'd meet up with him at different places. I don't remember where he came from; he just sort of appeared. He seemed friendly enough, although he had this weird stare. And, man, he spoke so loudly; he was an attention-seeker. I remember packing up and moving once before we moved into the main town, which was about twenty minutes away, to live with him. I can't recall why we did that. Looking back, it was likely because Mum and Dad's divorce was finalising. Kids weren't told about anything back then and we wouldn't dare ask. I never had any closure with Dad. He was there and then he wasn't. It was a really strange feeling.

As kids, we just did what we were told. I was still quite young when we moved, and I don't really remember my older siblings being around much. My eldest sibling, my sister, was ten years older than me. One of my brothers was seven years older and the other was two years older than me. My eldest brother went and lived with Dad in the valley and my sister went somewhere else at some point. She had a boyfriend at the time and was always with him.

So, when we moved to Beauy, it felt like it may just have been Mum, her new man, my youngest brother and me. The picture of the house we moved into is still etched in my memory. It was a Queenslander on concrete stilts in the middle of town, just up from the post office. Old door handles, wooden floors, free-standing cupboards and dusty with creaks in every corner.

Dark, cold, scary.

The events that transpired while we lived that house changed my life forever. It was the start of a roller-coaster childhood filled with fear, paranormal activity, chaos and confusion. Years later, I realised why I'd started misbehaving. I'd been bloody scared for so long. Plus, I was so fucking angry. That house was where I first started having nightmares – ones I vividly remembered the next morning. Ones where you feel like you don't sleep at all. Full-body, numbing terrors. I started having them every damn night and I hated it. They felt real; they were the in-your-face kind of nightmares.

Senses, shadows, vibrations.

I'd sense things around me and feel vibrations beneath my feet. Even when I woke up, it was like I was still dreaming.

I think I've always been a bit sensitive. I didn't feel like I really had much going for me – I wasn't sporty or pretty or popular among kids my age. I used to cry a lot. My stepdad – not that he was my stepdad at that time – closed my bedroom door at night. Sometimes he locked it! He was such a prick. He had to have everything a certain way. Worse, it felt like Mum was never home. My brother and I had to spend many afternoons with him after school, and we very quickly learned not to talk back or interrupt him in any way. If we did, we copped it.

My stepdad was tall and dominating – and I was shit-scared. He'd stalk us with his eyes. If I had to turn my back or walk past him for anything, I'd just be waiting for a thump as I went by. Sometimes, as I moved closer, he'd just yell a word to scare me. I began to see a side of him that wasn't quite right. I was still little but I knew he was off.

My brother and I spoke about it all the time. From the time we were eight or nine, we were plotting escape routes from our life. I used to sneak into my brother's room at night just to feel safe, and so I didn't have to be alone in my room with the sounds – let alone the nightmares. Every night I'd ask Mum to leave the light on, and she would. But then my stepdad would get up and turn it off. He knew I was scared. And he knew about the nightmares too. He didn't care. To him, I was just some kid screaming out at night. He used to tell me I was 'wasting electricity'.

The other thing he liked to do was keep my brother and I separated. This meant that whenever we'd go into each other's room for anything – day or night – we had to be so quiet. If we weren't, he'd come in and reef us out. Then he'd throw us back into our rooms and shut the door.

My room was so big – those old Queenslanders were all the same back then – and all I had was a single bed, a cupboard and these fine, white curtains that covered the stained windows. The floors would creak when I went to the toilet at night. I perfected the route so as not to wake my stepdad. Sometimes, though, I'd just hold it in to save the anxiety, but that would only work for so long.

All my nightmares centred around darkness, aliens and visions of things not from this world. I'd dream about getting away from him too – running, hiding. It was crippling. I had no idea what the hell was happening around me, and he always acted like we were doing something wrong or mischievous, intentionally, just to piss him off. We were just small children for Christ sakes.

At some point, we ended up with a puppy. Getting a dog was the only good thing to come from that place. Jake was so cute and the best company, but he was a Bull Terrier and he'd get so bored. My stepfather was garden-mad and didn't want Jake roaming around the yard, so he'd chain him up under the house while we were out. Jake was a puppy and still had his sharp little teeth and inquisitive nature so, of course, he'd break the rules. He'd dig up the garden or pee under the house during the day. I mean, what was he supposed to do? My stepdad would flog that dog – and then some. The sound of a yelping dog never leaves you.

Poor Jake had a terrible time of it; he ended up getting hit by a car and we lost him. We had other dogs, growing up, and my stepdad was cruel – intentional and mean – to all of them.

Sometimes, my stepdad would have an 'episode'. This meant having a fight with Mum. The fights were usually over us because we were 'the problem'. That's what we'd be told. If it wasn't us, he'd be mad at the dog or some other bullshit. I'd go into a bit of a trance when him and Mum started yelling. I'd zone out and hold my breath. Or I'd wait to make a run for it – over to the car if Mum decided we were going to leave.

Eventually, we moved back to Tamrookum; to the house Dad and Mum had originally built for the family when they were still together. Dad was living in Kooralbyn by this time, and Mum had decided she was getting married to this guy.

I could never understand how most people just had it figured out. Some people even just seemed to have a life that was normal – in my eyes anyway. Most of the kids at school had no life dramas that I could see. If they did, it didn't show. Their parents were all involved in school stuff – the mum of one of my mates was a teacher aide, and she doubled as the tuckshop lady and receptionist.

My school had forty-eight kids from Years 1 through to 7. It's hard to imagine now. Mum was usually working, and Dad never came to anything put on at the school. There are actually big chunks of primary school I just don't remember. Actually, there are chunks missing from my childhood – all over the place. I don't remember celebrating birthdays or anniversaries, or anything else like that.

How does everyone else replay memories verbatim?

Our stepdad kept us away from Mum as much as possible. It was the 80s, and he'd say, "Kids are to be seen and not heard!" I always hated hearing that saying as a kid. *Fuck off* I used to think. Dad swore a lot, so I'd known the choice words early on. That word became one of my favourites. *Fuck off!* I just wanted to spend time with Mum. Mother's Day was the one day of the year we could be with Mum all day – without needing an excuse. There was ALWAYS an argument on Mother's Day. Our stepdad had no excuses; she was our mum, not his.

Looking back, I think Mum was exhausted. She lacked the physicality, and the emotional presence she – we – needed.

By the time I was seven, I had a regular routine. It was, of course, woven together alongside my stepdad's outlandish outbursts, threats, random abuse, name calling – the list goes on. It was shit.

The last Mother's Day I can recall was when I was around eight or nine. The morning was a bit of a blur; we weren't allowed to sleep past 7 am so we were up early. I think we were planning to go to Kooralbyn for a swim. He never wanted to go, and we were fine with that. Mum could never be herself around him anyway. We could tell – and she knew we didn't like him. He was very possessive towards Mum – especially on Mother's Day or if Mum was unwell. Mum used to get terrible migraines so the locum would give her a pethidine shot and she'd be out for hours. Our stepdad would hide her away and lock us outside so we couldn't get in or be near her.

I recall one time I snuck inside to get water and something to eat – and he caught me. He scared the shit out of me and chased me out the back door. We were always on edge around him; we never knew what was coming. He was so predictable but equally as unpredictable. He had weird shit, like all parents do, but his was fucked up.

Dictatory, mean, controlling.

I did what I could to not piss him off – until I didn't. That day – Mother's Day – him and Mum started arguing and I remember running out the bedroom sliding door and down the front path to the car, which was parked by the shed. He was running after us. Mum was yelling and so was he. All I could think was that I just needed to get in the car and lock it before he caught up. I was scared he'd get to Mum before we could leave.

He was so mad that day, but then he stopped. He just stood there in the middle of the front yard and stared at us as we drove out. He was a crazy fucker. We lived on two acres, on the Mount Lindesay Highway. I was looking out the back window right through until the Kooralbyn turn-off, hoping he wasn't following us. My heart was racing the whole time, but we made it. We ended up swimming all afternoon at the pool.

Then, we had to go back home.

We always had to go back and I never knew what we'd be walking into. Sometimes it was like nothing had happened. He'd come and greet Mum and pretend everything was okay. Other times, I thought he was going to kill us all. My brother and I knew he had a twenty-two in the cupboard and we'd agreed that if he started to hit Mum, we'd shoot him. I had to stay close to my brother most of the time, even though I knew he couldn't help me – he was four-foot-nothing, just like me, but he tried.

Every day seemed to go on forever. Once I was old enough to understand the dynamics of our home life and how to navigate a tiny school in the middle of nowhere, I became hyper-aware of everything. Every sound, every movement. If someone's face or posture changed, I'd notice and alter mine to fit the situation. That was until I didn't care enough anymore and decided to rebel.

No-one knew what it was like at home. Parents didn't talk about their kids and kids didn't talk about their parents. I remember getting busted with a West Coast Cooler in Grade 5. I'd taken it to school and was drinking it with my mates. I was so dumb. The teachers found the bottle in the bin and someone dobbed on me.

I wasn't popular at school – popular girls played netball – but I did have a few close friends. We were surrounded by farmland, so every so often I'd go to a mate's dairy farm over the hill and we'd ride around on her four-wheelers or help in the milking shed. We used to fill massive cups with about ten scoops of Milo, then go out to the cold milk vat and pour it straight into our cups. That was the best milk I've ever tasted. We didn't stay friends for long though because she started going out with a guy I liked. She was a year older than me and much more mature – that's what it seemed like to me, anyway.

Life went on. I hated school. All I wanted was to fit in and find my place.

When I was eleven, I had a best friend who lived further out bush than we did. She and I caught different buses home but a few times I was allowed to go for a sleepover. We'd hang out and do dumb shit. Her parents were way cooler than mine. She didn't have a bedtime and we could pretty much do whatever we wanted. One weekend I stayed over and we slept in a caravan in the block next to their place. It seemed like fun at the time. I remember waking up five or six times to pee that particular night. We were a fair way from the main house and I'd have to jump the fence, so each time I just squatted on the grass instead.

I knew something wasn't right – needing to pee so much – but I didn't think it was anything major. I'd lost a bit of weight. I'd been a chubby kid growing up and used food as an emotional support. Now, though, I wanted to be skinnier. I didn't care how I got there either. It felt so good to be like my friends and not be 'the fat girl'. Boys took notice of me at school and didn't talk to me like I was an alien.

I started to get worse though.

I was drinking litres and litres of anything I could get my hands on – the thirst just wouldn't go away – and I'd pee it out soon after. Little did I know that my body had been attacking itself and the cells in my pancreas were undergoing major damage. I didn't even know what a pancreas was.

Not too long later, Mum took me to the local GP one afternoon and he did a blood glucose test by pricking my finger. My level was twenty-five! Normally, people sit around five. That day, I was diagnosed with Type 1 Juvenile Diabetes.

Within a few hours, I was on my way to the Children's Hospital in Brisbane. I was admitted and hooked up to monitors. I was there for about four or five days, I think. They educated me on what diabetes was and how I had to look after myself from now on – forever. Daily injections, finger pricking – they even taught me how to draw up insulin from a vial. The food I could eat every day now had to be portion-controlled.

Seriously!

I'd spent the best part of my earlier years battling with my self-confidence because I was bigger than all my friends. I'd had times when food was withheld at home until we asked for something to eat because we were hungry. I'd also been belittled daily by my stepfather about being fat and 'always eating'. And now I was being told I had to count the portions of my food and only have so much, at certain times!

I remember thinking that I would not follow this plan. I'd do what I wanted. I was pre-pubescent. Like my friends, I felt like I was older than I really was. I'd spent the last five years witnessing countless, horrific moments at the hands of my stepfather. My brother and I had grown up very quickly. We'd had to, and we'd both developed dangerous minds and sixth senses.

For me, this news about the diabetes was a turning point. It was like I'd been scooped up and taken straight into my early teens.

FULL THROTTLE!

Where I'd already been had nothing on where I was going.

Born in rural Queensland in the early 1980s, **KM** *grew up navigating the complexities of a small-town childhood shaped by family dysfunction, paranormal frequencies and personal health challenges. These experiences shaped a heightened sensitivity to multi-dimensional energies and psychic downloads – tools that would later become vital to personal survival and self-discovery. After moving to the Gold Coast as a teenager in the late '90s, KM's life spiralled into parties, substance abuse, early independence and near-death experiences. Becoming a young parent brought grounding, and for over twenty-five years, KM has called the Sunshine Coast home. This chapter is an extract from her debut memoir and offers a raw and poignant glimpse into her youth – growing up in the bush, navigating her parents' divorce, and confronting a lifelong health condition at a young age. Through it all, her journey is one of determination, resilience and intuition.*

The Mirror I Refused to Look Into

Melissa Wilkes

I think the first time I realised just how much my childhood had impacted my life was about fifteen years ago.

I was on the phone to a friend, talking about some problems I was having. I was venting, feeling stuck. This was before people were really having these kinds of conversations. Before podcasts and therapists and Instagram quotes about childhood trauma were a thing.

I remember my friend saying to me, "You really need to go and see someone. Like a specialist… a psychologist."

And my first thought? Gee, thanks. So you're saying I'm crazy? Funnily enough, she is no longer a friend – but not because of that.

The idea of going back through my childhood … it felt dangerous. It felt like it would open doors I couldn't close. Like it would unleash things I wasn't ready to face. I thought it would expose me to a level of vulnerability I didn't want anything to do with. The fear it created in me was huge. It felt unnecessary. Ridiculous. I wanted nothing to do with it.

So instead, I started studying nutrition.

That felt safer. Cleaner.

And while I was doing that, I started hearing little bits about personal development. That felt more approachable than seeing a psych, so I jumped in.

Back then, personal development wasn't what it is now. Sure, there were murmurs of Tony Robbins, but it wasn't mainstream. Even when I became a coach ten years ago, most people didn't know what a 'coach' was. It's wild how much can change in just a decade.

One thing I learned pretty quickly about personal development is that you don't get to avoid the past. You can try, but eventually it finds you.

Now, here's the part that used to really annoy me about people who were 'doing the work' on their childhood ... the whole idea of *blaming*. I judged it hard. I rolled my eyes. *What's the point of blaming your parents?* I thought.

Yet, when I started doing the work myself ... I realised I was full of blame.

Full of blame for the experiences I didn't have. Blame for the love I didn't feel from my mother.

Blame for the affection that never came. Blame for the safety I didn't get to feel.

So there I was, judging other people for something I was completely consumed by.

Halfway through this journey, with the help of a coach, I finally started to see the truth. I was angry. Not annoyed. Not irritated.

Angry. Rage lived inside me. Hate. Hurt. It was like it had embedded itself in my skin. I walked it. Talked it. Breathed it. It was everywhere.

And here's the thing ... I was married. I had three amazing kids. Had I projected all of that pain onto them? Had I passed it on without even knowing?

That realisation shook me.

Then another truth hit me – I'd created this illusion in my mind that I was perfect. That I was *right*. I had a kind of self-righteous streak. If you wanted to argue with me back then, good luck. I didn't back down. I'd bring facts, fiction, prophecies – anything to win. I *had* to be right. Why? Because if I wasn't perfect, people may see the 'other parts' of me.

So, how does a woman who thinks she's right, avoids her pain and carries quiet fury in her bones end up with a loving family?

I still don't really know.

What I do know is this: what came next was shame.

Shame is such an interesting emotion. Out of all the things we can feel, I think shame is the one that will truly stop you in your tracks. You can't move forward when you're drowning in it. When it keeps popping up in your mind, it's paralysing.

That's where everything shifted for me.

The anger and hurt from my childhood wasn't just about the experiences. It was about *who* those experiences came from. Someone who was meant to love me. Protect me. Keep me safe. All I'd ever told myself, growing up, was that I wasn't going to be anything like her.

And yet ... here I was.

My thoughts, my feelings, my behaviours – they weren't all that different. And I'd projected them onto the people I love the most – my kids and my husband. In arguments. In insecurity. I'd projected them at work when someone challenged me. I'd projected them with friends when I'd felt judged. It was like the shame had become a pain in my gut. A physical sensation. It didn't lead me into depression, thankfully, but it did start shaping who I was.

Do you know when that ugly part of me would come out most?

When I drank alcohol.

Personal development is like holding a mirror up to yourself. You can't hide anymore. You start to see what's been buried. What's been shoved down, ignored and denied. When you see it – really see it – it's confronting.

What's hiding inside?

For me, it was the parts of me I didn't want to admit existed. The ugly, angry, bitter parts. The mean voice. The sharp tongue. The control. The shame.

Back then, I hadn't realised that everyone has something. Everyone's been through something that left a scar. A moment of embarrassment. Humiliation. Something they regret. A time they messed up. A mistake they haven't forgiven themselves for.

But I didn't know that then.

I thought I was the *only one* who had this darkness. This shame. This side of me I hated. This part I couldn't show.

She wasn't nice.

She was angry. She was bitter. She was a bitch.

She was my mother.

And she was me!

As a child, my weekends were mostly spent at my grandparents' property just outside the city. They had geese, ducks, fruit trees, a vegetable garden, big trees and space to run. At my Nannan's – that's what I called her instead of 'Nanna' – I was encouraged to just be me.

I'd dance around the lounge. Make up plays she had to watch. Sing out loud. Eat when I was hungry; stop when I was full. No-one shamed me with 'there are kids starving in Africa'. I'd dress up in costumes, wear Nannan's clip-on earrings, parade around like I owned the place.

For a while, I did. That place was mine. I felt safe. Loved. Seen. Heard. It was a vast, vast contrast to how I felt at home during the week.

It became my sanctuary – until I was twelve.

That's when my grandparents separated. My grandad was suddenly just ... gone. I never saw him again. It was like a piece of my safety net had been yanked away without warning.

I remember one day, maybe a year later, asking Mum why I was dropped at Nannan's every weekend. She finally told me – during an argument: "Because you were too much. I couldn't handle you. I still can't."

Just like that, the puzzle clicked into place.

I flashed back to a moment when I was about six. My brother was four. He wasn't staying with me at Nannan's that weekend, it was just me. I remember playing quietly nearby and overhearing a conversation between my mum and Nannan.

Nannan asked, "Why aren't you letting your son come too? Why just her?"

Mum said something like, "It's just her I have the problem with. She doesn't shut up. She's too much. She's naughty too."

Then Nannan said, "You don't seem like you've bonded with her."

Mum replied, "I haven't. Sometimes I get angry just looking at her."

I don't think I even knew what those words meant at the time, but I *felt* them. And I carried them with me from that moment on.

Those feelings shaped the thoughts I had about myself. The behaviours I adopted. The shame I carried. That was the moment I started becoming someone else. Someone acceptable. Someone less. Someone quieter.

Now, as an adult, I understand Mum was just repeating the same story her mum wrote for her. I get it now. I've done the work. I can see the cycle.

But that doesn't help the little girl I was.

It doesn't erase the confusion. The ache. The quiet longing for a cuddle that never came. There are photos of Mum hugging me when I was very young, but none after a certain age. It's like the affection just stopped.

As a parent myself, I get how impossible and messy parenting can be. We don't get manuals. No-one warns you what might show up if you experienced trauma or rejection growing up.

But I've learned something powerful. Something personal. If you grow up feeling unloved or unwanted – even if it's not loud or obvious – it *does* affect you. It impacts in more ways than you can ever explain. If you've never felt that, if you were lucky enough to feel loved and safe growing up, you'll never fully understand what it's like.

You can listen. You can care. You can empathise. But you'll never really know.

After all the pain, all the unravelling, all the shame and work and heartbreak, I've finally come to this:

Everything I needed as a child… I can give to myself now.

And that's something I get to control.

Melissa Wilkes *is a Nutrition and Mindset Coach who helps women break free from emotional and binge eating, body struggles and the exhausting cycle of dieting. Through her* Life Upgrade *program, she supports women to heal their relationship with food and themselves without restriction, calorie counting or guilt. A wife and mum of three, Melissa is also an avid adventure-seeker who runs soul-nourishing retreats for women overseas. She's equally obsessed with green juice and a cheeky rosé on a sunny Saturday. After doing the deep work to heal her own pain and patterns, she's now passionate about helping other women live healthier, happier lives with more self-love, more confidence and way less stress.*

Embracing and Empowering the Sacred Feminine

Maria Solano

The shattering of self began in utero.

I entered a world where the men in the family were to always be obeyed and enabled, and the women were not allowed to have a voice.

In December 1972, my mother drove herself home from the hospital after my birth. At the time, my father was nearby, at the family business he owned with my mother. My grandfather had started the business in 1951 when my father's family arrived in Australia from Sicily. My parents met through Mum's auntie, who later married Dad's older brother. Years later, I found out that this auntie had betrayed my mother by having a longstanding affair with my father. This affair started when Mum was pregnant with me.

The business kept us clothed, fed and comfortable. Annual island and snow trips, Catholic school education, sports and dance weekends. It was also the business that provided the perfect alibi for the ongoing secret life that Dad undertook.

The absent father routine was mostly a blessing. Having my father at home meant scrambling to make sure the house was in perfect order when we heard his car wheels hit the grate in the drive. The few times a week he was home for dinner was a gut-clenching affair, silent except for Dad's shouting, throwing of beer cans or fist-thumps on my bedroom door because I hadn't put a board game away. I spent that time – when a family comes together to eat and share their day – rocking back and forth in my chair, self-soothing. Fear became embedded deep in my being. My father's voice became the voice that drove my nightmares, my apprehension and my anxiety. The act of eating became a shameful activity for me as it was tied heavily to guilt. Years later, I still suffer from multiple digestive issues.

I developed early – at the age of ten – and was bullied by girls who would try to rip my uniform off my shoulders and harass me in the toilets to see if I had my period. By the time I was thirteen, I'd slimmed down and my curves were in proportion, but I still saw myself as that overweight, undesirable girl who would never be as slim as the other girls. For most of my life, my weight has fluctuated between sizes six and twelve, and I have many food intolerances. Ironically enough, I trained as a chef when I finished high school. I had no great passion for food; I think it was more of an emotional choice. I felt I needed to get my fear of food under control.

Mum's focus was on keeping Dad happy. He'd say to me, "You're good for nothing, where did I go wrong?" Mum heard him but said nothing. Her silence confirmed that I was no good. It was my fault

I was being yelled at and so began the people-pleasing. Everyone else deserved better than – more than – me.

Don't worry about me. I'll be okay.

No, really... I'm not okay.

Why do I have a voice if I'm not allowed to use it?

I'm ugly. I'm useless. I'm nothing.

I developed this set of messages and repeated them to myself often. They shaped my childhood, my core beliefs and my psyche.

At no point did I think the way I was being raised was normal or okay. I had an inner wisdom beyond my years that understood, at an abstract level, that this was not what love was. I'd notice when my mother would disconnect from her body. I could hear it in her voice and see it in her face, especially her eyes. It made me anxious. It made me feel unsafe. Even though I didn't use my outside voice for fear of betrayal and rejection, my inner voice stood by my side, took my hand and said, "I am always here for you."

My first crush was on the son of Mum's best friend. I was twelve. Mum and her best friend would take us to our house in the mountains to ski every winter school holidays. My crush just happened to be the most popular boy at school and my adoration for him shone bright. He found this amusing and teased me constantly. As we went through school together, he would take me to parties and try to get me to smoke and drink like the other cool kids. For me, experimenting wasn't worth the repercussions and punishment I'd receive if I ever got found out. So, I was always the outcast. I never fit in.

When my father was in the house, I wasn't allowed in the same room as another male my age. One time we were playing hide and seek at my house and my crush was hiding in my room. Dad came to my door and asked if he was in there. I said no. Later, when I was found out, Dad slapped me across the face and locked me in my room while the others continued their game. I can still feel the sting; the raised ridges of those hands in anger. The hands that supposedly held me close as a baby. The hands that then betrayed me as a child.

The control and the manipulation meant shaping my personality became very difficult. I was not standing in my power at any point in those years, and I had no-one to talk to about the way I felt. I couldn't communicate with men at all, so I became very defensive when they spoke to me. It was safer to reject them before they rejected me. My outlet at this time was communicating my feeling by writing. Writing short stories, notes to my friends, in my journal.

My brother was afforded different standards to myself as my mother had been taught that men were infinitely more important than women, and that women were here to care for men. Therefore, my brother was given an abundance of freedom. It was made clear to me that sex and intimacy were off limits, so when I received my first kiss at the age of seventeen, it was a passionless, awkward moment.

As soon as school was over, I began looking for employment. I got my driver's licence and was still living at home. As Dad was usually at work till the early hours of the morning, I could go out after my chef shifts to dance and see my friends, and I'd still get home before he did.

I love dancing. It's the one activity where I can lose myself completely in the moment. I expressed myself by moving my body, conveying my joy and freedom in the undulating rhythm of music and movement. In those days, drinks were cheap and gave me the confidence to speak to men. As long as the drink high lasted, I was confident, fun and laid back.

When I was twenty-one, I began my first romantic relationship. He was eighteen and much more experienced than me. Our union was intense as drama was habitual to me. I didn't know how to have a healthy relationship. We were engaged within six months, even though

I'd never wanted to get married. I'd seen what marriage entailed – it was a prison. I didn't show my partner affection when he visited, as my father saw us kissing once and told me my behaviour was disgusting. That relationship lasted for thirteen years. Ultimately, though, I let him go to have his own family while I worked on my avoidant attachment issues.

When I was twenty-five, I did a three-week coach tour of Europe. Most of my co-travellers were between the ages of fifty and sixty. I loved conversing about art and history with them. On a public water taxi in Venice, I danced down the aisle while an Italian man played his accordion on his way home from work. I danced around restaurants in Rome and a waiter swept me up onto a chair while a guitarist sang beside me. I stood barefoot on large stones in the Yorkshire Dales while wild horses ran circles around me. I began to experience who the real me was – away from all the constraints and conditions.

By this time, I'd trained in administration and was working for the Director of Psychiatry as her executive assistant. My boss was a woman of forty with a no-nonsense, terse approach. Her demeanour made more sense to me when she disclosed that, on her first day, one of the male doctors said, "We never wanted you here." Hearing that, I could appreciate that her manner was one of a need to prove herself to a workplace that was dominated by men.

A few years later, I was working as a personal assistant for the Supreme Court and developed glandular fever, which then turned into chronic fatigue syndrome. I started needing twice-weekly doctor's appointments to receive vitamin infusions, injections and plasma. There was a lot of judgement and verbal abuse from my family during this time. As my illness progressed, my friends started distancing themselves from me as I wasn't able to drive anymore or go out socially very often.

During this time my kinesiologist tapped on my upper arm muscle and said, "Your mum believed your father didn't love her when you were six months old." I asked Mum about this and the whole story of Dad's affair with my aunt came flooding out. When I was six months old, my auntie broke off the affair and my father tried to kill himself with a pill overdose.

My mum's trauma transferred to me. I became fascinated with the whole brain/body connection and this began my lifetime of delving into the emotions and thoughts we experience and how they impact on our physical body.

At thirty-two, I found out I was pregnant. On one hand, I was ecstatic. But, I was also fearful of how I would physically and energetically take care of this precious life. I'd had a major car accident when I was twenty-five and sustained slipped discs, a traumatic brain injury and post-traumatic stress disorder (PTSD). My partner liked to drink a lot. He also had a temper, and I wanted to be able to nurture and protect my child in the way I wasn't.

I decided I was prepared to raise this child as a single mother.

Six weeks into my pregnancy I had an ultrasound. It showed my baby wasn't developing as fast as it should and its heartbeat was too slow. At nine weeks I started spotting and went for another scan. Struggling to breathe, I listened to that heartbeat and looked at that body the size of a cherry with limbs forming. I cried for my baby and, later that night when he passed out of my body, I felt a part of my soul go with him.

I was encouraged to come into work the next morning and my people-pleasing mind said, "Okay." A few hours later, I was in emergency, haemorrhaging steadily.

Years later, I had a palm reading. The reader asked, "What happened when you were almost thirty-two? You almost died." It's true. I'd spent the night in hospital and my parents decided not to visit me – not in the hospital, and not when I was back home either. My partner coped by going out, getting drunk, driving home and saying to me, "Oh boo hoo, you don't have a baby. Why don't' you get a dog?"

I struggled on at work until I couldn't. My illness had gotten worse. I couldn't get the disability pension because my partner earned more than $300 a week, even though most of his money went to his disabled parents. My mother had discovered my father's latest mistress and asked him to move out of the house; he'd told her to get over it.

It had all come to a head: I was jobless, my parents were broken and my relationship was pretty much over. I couldn't do much about the first two, but I could fix the third. I ended my relationship and bunkered down in my apartment for the next year.

As it turned out, I couldn't afford to keep my apartment, so I moved three hours away to a town I'd visited once. Three months later, I woke up to find an intruder in my bedroom. When he noticed I was awake, he jumped up from the end of my bed and ran out of the room. He'd taken my mobile phone, but thankfully I was able to get to a landline. My guitar and camera were also missing. Memories were now gone forever. My sense of safety demolished.

The trauma basically tipped me over the edge. I'd prop a chair in front of the door and make myself stay awake until the sun came up. I didn't care if I walked in front of a bus and was killed. I felt like I'd had no break from one challenge to the next, and my body and mind were overwhelmed. I went fully into victim mode.

My new partner had Asperger's and took my behaviour personally, unable to deal with my fluctuating emotions. I didn't know at the time, but he was an alcoholic and his drinking worsened after the incident. For his part, he didn't realise my reaction was thirty years in the making.

I had to turn this torment around. To this point, I'd gotten through life with strength and willpower, living in survive or thrive. Now it was time to thrive.

Growing up, I'd been very physical. I'd played a lot of sports and danced six nights a week. Now I had to find an outlet that wasn't so physical or demanding on my exhausted and damaged body.

I joined a psychic development circle and started to see an herbalist who specialised in EFT (a tapping technique for emotional freedom). I asked my partner to move out as his addictions were taking too much of my focus and energy. We'd been together for nine years but it wasn't my job to fix him. I wasn't here to be his mother or to put up with his tantrums. For me, it was incredibly important that I maintain my own independence and sense of self, even with a partner. Now I've learned to feel whole and complete without a partner or even dating. It has been this way for the last eight years.

I made a number of new friends, but it was impossible for me to obtain the level of intimacy I desired. With my illness and injuries, I had to strictly pace myself, resting and scheduling outings with careful planning. Friendships that started off well would always reach the point where I'd be cast aside for other friends who were more spontaneous and energetic. I was also very honest – an open book – which could make people uncomfortable.

But – being away from my family was liberating. I finally felt like I had a voice. And I was determined to use it!

During lockdown, I studied online at university. I learned the ukulele. I got back into my painting. Growing up, I'd been told my artwork was naive and not great, but as I gained self-confidence, my ability to be resilient and rise above the opinions and judgements of others increased. I started exhibiting my work at galleries and writing stories for books. Last year, I studied as a priestess, releasing more trauma and re-connecting with the powerful divine goddess I'd been all along. Through all my life experiences, I've gained wisdom, learned how to self-regulate my nervous system, and cleared traumas from this lifetime as well as past lifetimes.

I've reclaimed my power as a worthy, deserving, authentic being.

I've started living my life purpose.

Our Shadow Self

As we grow up, we learn patterns from our parents, teachers, primary caregivers and friends. They shape us. Sometimes, we have to sacrifice who we really are – or were meant to become – to keep the peace, fit in and feel worthy or loved. In doing this, we potentially abandon the part of ourselves that needs to feel safe, supported and accepted. This leads to a lack of self-worth, self-confidence, guilt and shame – all feelings that don't make us feel good about ourselves and that have an impact on where we allow life to lead us. We see hidden meaning in situations due to our learned interpretation, and we react accordingly.

It's important that we learn to be objective and separate the facts from the feelings by observing the feeling and sitting with it instead of jumping to conclusions. Take time to sit in that space, breathe and let the emotion go. Get into your body and breathe into your heart.

Self-love and Self-care

Healthy self-worth appears in our lives as peace within. It allows us to make our own decisions without needing approval or acceptance from others. We have healthy boundaries, and work through challenges with resilience and grace.

Have compassion for yourself. You are not the patterns that you created from the messages you received.

Re-parent yourself if you need to. This was a big issue for me. I didn't receive the nurturing I needed in childhood, which caused all sorts of problems going into adulthood. However, I learned I could give myself the reassurance and safety I never felt.

Take that inner child's hand, look deep into her eyes and say, "I love you. I see you and I am here for you." Give her a big hug. She is the 'you' that had all the dreams and the wishes. She is the innocent and pure soul that started her journey on this Earth with so much hope and happiness. You can be her. You are her. Sometimes we have to lose people in our lives to find ourselves, and to love ourselves. We cannot take responsibility for everyone else's journey.

Self-compassion

What messages do you tell yourself? Do you judge yourself as you may have been
 judged? If you do this right, will people love you and accept you?

Working from a set of false beliefs that aren't really yours will only make you miserable. The pain of acting a certain way to please others or the need to feel validated is exhausting.

As women, historically we have taken on the role as caregiver to children, aging parents, and even partners – and we've put ourselves last. What can you do today to be kind to yourself? What can you do to extend compassion and care to 'you' rather than just giving to others?

Your needs are just as important as anybody else's. Show up for yourself as a strong, powerful woman who deserves happiness, success and love in her life. Come home to yourself and feel complete in your self-love. Be present in this moment with your thoughts, your emotions, your actions and your words – and change the way you talk to yourself.

Do you have limiting self-talk?

Your brain can't tell the difference between what you think and what is actually happening. If you think about all the things that could possibly go wrong, and then live in fear and anxiety, your body and brain will respond in kind, which can lead to all sorts of mental and physical problems. When you learn to heal all parts of yourself, you come back to the divine feminine being you were always meant to be.

Integration of Self

Acknowledge just how incredible you are and how joyous life is meant to be while you're experiencing it. Women have spent lifetimes being undervalued, not being taken seriously, being seen as second best and being disempowered. It is our time to shine our light and take back our magnificent power. Become grounded in your truth and in your body. Listen to your wisdom. You don't need to second-guess yourself because when you trust your intuition, you don't need external approval.

Stand tall in your authenticity – your beautiful feminine essence – rather than shrinking to fit in. Be the leader in your life. Flow with the challenges. Roar when you need to. Be soft when required.

Create a life for yourself that is in alignment with your values, showcases your gifts and makes you feel excited.

Accept the good things you are offered – you deserve it! Women have been buried under too much shit for too long. The world needs all of us to stand together as a sacred sisterhood where we have each other's backs and, more importantly, have our own backs.

Your dreams are not impossible – and don't let anyone tell you otherwise. Even if you don't achieve all your dreams, just believe in yourself and your capabilities, and many more opportunities will come your way.

The next chapter of your life starts now.

Make it extraordinary.

Maria Solano *is a writer, artist and photographer who live with two sassy rabbits, Gypsy and Merlin. Over the last fifteen years, she has collaborated in various creative pursuits, namely non-fiction books on healing, empaths, art exhibitions and photography magazines. Maria lives for reading, nature, rescue animals, live music and a breathtaking view in whatever part of the world she can get to.*

"We don't have to live forever; we just have to live."

From Breakdown to a New Blueprint

Anne Barratt

There was a time in my life when everything felt like it was quietly slipping through my fingers. Not in one big dramatic moment, but more like a slow and steady loss of the life I thought I was supposed to have. From the outside, things looked fine. I had built a strong career in marketing. I was responsible, capable and doing what was expected of me. But deep down, something always felt like it didn't quite fit.

Being the child of immigrants meant I learned how to adapt early. Estonian was my first language. I didn't realise I was different until I started going to daycare and school. I couldn't understand the other kids and they didn't understand me. I remember waking up from a nap at daycare once; the room was dark and quiet, and I had no idea what was happening or what the teacher was saying. I felt completely alone. I didn't have the words and I didn't feel safe. That moment stayed with me far longer than anyone around me would have known.

I picked up English quickly, but the feeling of not being enough, of not belonging, stuck around. I kept my circle small. I did what I could to fit in. I tried hard. Always trying to be good, trying to be liked, trying to be accepted. It became a habit I carried into adulthood, especially into my work. I became very good at looking like I had it all together, even when I didn't.

I didn't understand at the time just how much I had internalised. The emotional silence I grew up with, and the relentless pressure I later placed on myself, were slowly building into something I could no longer ignore.

Like many girls of my generation, growing up I was taught that children should be seen but not heard. Emotions weren't things we talked about. If I cried, I was told to stop. If I was angry, it was met with silence or discomfort. Nobody ever sat me down and explained that feelings were meant to be felt, processed, and released. I learned to hold them in.

At first, it just made me quiet. Obedient. A 'good girl'. But over time it made me anxious, disconnected and self-critical. I didn't know how to speak up for myself, even when something hurt. I learned early on to push things down and carry on. I became skilled at making things look fine on the outside, even when I was crumbling on the inside.

The bullying started in primary school. I was different. I didn't speak English fluently at first. I didn't understand the social cues. I was picked on, laughed at, left out. I didn't feel safe. It chipped away at my sense of self – layer by layer – until I learned to anticipate rejection before it even came. I developed a kind of emotional radar for who might be safe and who might turn on me. Even when the bullying stopped, the damage lingered. I still held that tightness in my chest; that need to prove I was enough.

That same pattern followed me into high school and then into my professional life. Even as I began to succeed on paper, there was always a part of me running on empty. In the corporate world, I excelled. I worked in marketing and communications, managing multi-million-dollar budgets, overseeing teams, launching national campaigns. I thrived under pressure – or so it seemed.

Underneath the performance was constant self-doubt, perfectionism and an overwhelming fear of failing. I worked long hours, often through weekends, chasing deadlines and approval in equal measure. I pushed through migraines, exhaustion and burnout, brushing off the signs that my body was waving in front of me like red flags. For over twenty years, I experienced chronic migraines. Sometimes they'd knock me flat, but more often I just worked through them, gritting my teeth and pushing harder.

Looking back, I can see how deeply I had internalised the idea that rest was weakness. That being emotional was messy. That asking for help meant I had failed. I didn't stop. I just kept adding more – more achievements, more qualifications, more certifications. I was always studying something. It gave me a sense of control and a sense of worthiness. If I wasn't enough as I was, maybe I could *become* enough through constant improvement.

The cost was high.

The stress built up in my body like a pressure cooker. There was nowhere for it to go. I didn't know how to express my pain, so my body expressed it for me. Inflammation became my body's language. Migraines were its alarm bells. Eventually, that stress manifested in deeper imbalances – hormonal issues, endometriosis, adrenal fatigue.

I now understand how all of it was connected. Not just physically or emotionally, but energetically. My nervous system had been stuck in survival mode for decades. Fight, flight, freeze. I didn't know peace. I didn't know how to feel safe *just being*. My body became the canvas where all of that unprocessed pain was painted.

When I discovered kinesiology, something shifted.

For the first time, I began to understand that emotions are not weaknesses. They are signals. They are energy that needs movement. Kinesiology taught me how to listen to my body, how to process old traumas, how to find where stuck emotions were held. It taught me how to gently begin to release them. It gave me a new language, not just for healing but for *wholeness*.

I realised that my symptoms weren't betrayals. They were messages. My body wasn't broken; it was communicating. Underneath the layers of stress, burnout and grief, there was still a part of me – quiet, steady, sacred – waiting to be heard.

That part of me wasn't chasing approval. She wasn't trying to be perfect. She was simply asking for space. To rest. To be. To feel.

And that's when I started making real changes. Not because I'd hit rock bottom but because I finally saw what was underneath it all. The emotional pain, the pressure, the constant striving – it had never been about proving myself to others. It was about healing the parts of me that had never been taught I was enough just as I am.

I had become so used to surviving, I forgot what it felt like to truly live in my body. But that was about to change.

Over time, my body started telling a different story. It began with small things – pain, discomfort, fatigue – but these grew. I went to doctors, over and over, but I wasn't really heard. The responses were often dismissive. I was told it was probably stress, or 'just part of being a woman'. I felt like I had to prove how bad it really was just to be taken seriously. After a long journey of searching, I was finally diagnosed with endometriosis.

The diagnosis was a relief and a punch in the gut at the same time. Finally, I had an answer – but that answer came with more questions, more pain and difficult decisions. The years that followed were filled with treatments and moments of hope that often turned into disappointment. Eventually, I had to make a decision that felt like the end of something important – I had a hysterectomy.

Letting go of the hope of becoming a mother was devastating. I had held onto that dream for so long. It was one of those quiet dreams – the kind you don't always speak out loud but live your life around anyway. I didn't just lose the ability to have a child; I lost the future I thought I was supposed to have.

There's a kind of grief that comes with this sort of loss that's hard to explain. There's no funeral. No recognition. People don't quite know what to say and they often say the wrong thing. "At least you can sleep in," or "You must have so much freedom." It didn't feel freeing. It felt like I had been left behind. Everyone around me seemed to be moving into the next season of life – having babies, raising children – while I was learning how to live with an emptiness that had no name.

And then came menopause.

Twice.

The first was forced on me after the surgery, before I was emotionally ready. The second, years later when it would have happened naturally. Both times left me feeling disconnected, not only from my body but from the world around me. It was as if life had fast-forwarded without me and I was still trying to catch my breath.

Those years were incredibly painful, but they were also the beginning of something I couldn't see at the time. Losing the life I thought I was meant to live made space for something else to grow. I didn't know it at the time but I was slowly uncovering a new version of myself – one that wasn't defined by ticking boxes or meeting expectations.

The old blueprint of my life had been torn apart, but maybe that was exactly what needed to happen. Maybe I wasn't here to follow a plan. Maybe I was here to draw a new one.

At first, I didn't know what rebuilding looked like. All I knew was that I couldn't go back to the way things were. Something inside me had shifted. I had lived through so much pain – emotional, physical, spiritual – and I had done most of it quietly. There were days when I questioned whether I had anything left to give but deep down a quiet whisper kept returning: *There has to be more than this.*

It didn't happen in a dramatic moment. The change came slowly, in layers. I began exploring different healing modalities – not because I planned to build a business but because I needed to find my way back to myself. I started with kinesiology, which opened me to a deeper understanding of how energy, emotion and the body are all connected. From there, I followed my curiosity and my intuition. I leaned into what resonated. Every new learning gave me a piece of myself back.

I realised something as I walked this path: I didn't want anyone else to feel as unseen or unsupported as I had during the hardest parts of my life. I wanted to help others in the way I had needed to be helped. That desire became the seed for *Empowering Health*. It wasn't a business idea; it was a soul decision. A commitment to offer others the kind of care, truth and space that had been missing from my own healing journey. I didn't want anyone to suffer in silence the way I had – or for as long as I had.

Around the same time, another part of me stirred to life – a part I hadn't expected to rise so strongly: the part that still longed to create. When I lost the chance to have children, something inside me still wanted to bring something meaningful into the world. I had this deep desire to pass something on; something beautiful, rooted, sacred. And that's how my Baltic Folk jewellery 'side-hustle' was born.

It started from a place of reverence. As I reconnected with my Estonian heritage, I was drawn to the ancient symbols and stories passed down through generations. Each one carried meaning: protection, guidance, transformation, balance, divine feminine strength. These weren't just designs to me, they were a language. They gave voice to the parts of me that had no words. They connected me back to a lineage of women who, like me, had carried pain, strength and beauty all at once.

What began as a spark became something much bigger – a passion project that filled me with joy and purpose. It became a way to honour my ancestors and share their wisdom with the modern world. More than that, it has become a living legacy. A way to pass something meaningful on to my goddaughter. She became my inspiration and my business partner. Creating the jewellery allowed me to share stories with her that might otherwise have been lost. It gave me an alternative sense of mothering, not in the traditional sense but in the most heartfelt, soul-led way.

This project didn't drain me. It nourished me. It reminded me that even in the face of grief we are still capable of creating beauty. Even when life doesn't go to plan, we can still find ways to birth something meaningful into the world. The jewellery wasn't just art, it was healing. It was a reminder that I hadn't failed, I had simply taken a different path – one that still allowed me to give, to teach and to leave a mark.

Empowering Health and *Baltic Folk* were not separate. They were both born from the same fire; the same choice to turn pain into purpose. One allowed me to hold space for others. The other allowed me to create something lasting, something tangible and something sacred.

Together, they reminded me I was never truly broken; I was just being reshaped into someone new.

The early years of *Empowering Health* were filled with heart. I was doing work I believed in, helping others find their way back to themselves just as I was trying to do for myself. As the years went on, however, the layers of grief and fatigue I had tried to manage began to surface again in ways I couldn't ignore.

When I launched *Baltic Folk*, it wasn't just a business. It was a creation born from love – a way to honour my Estonian roots, my inner spark and the maternal energy I had nowhere else to pour. It felt like a new kind of birth. A joy. Designing jewellery that carried sacred ancestral symbolism gave me something to hold onto; something that felt deeply meaningful. For a time, it filled a space in me that had long been empty.

When our first Australian manufacturer failed us – first by not delivering on time for our business launch and then by revealing they had misquoted us by tens of thousands of dollars – it shattered something inside me. We had already invested so much – time, money, energy, hope. It felt like a miscarriage. That might sound dramatic to some but that's exactly what it felt like – another promise of life lost before it had a chance to grow. It triggered the pain I thought I had made peace with, the deep, silent ache of childlessness. This time, however, it was tied to something I had *built*. Once again, I was left to face the emptiness.

Not long after, I lost my mum.

I had lost my father six years earlier but this was different. It was final. It was total. I was an only child and now I had no parents left. No safety net. No-one in the world who remembered my first words or the sound of my childhood laugh. The grief of losing my mother was deeper and sharper than I expected. It cracked open everything I thought I had processed about loss.

I didn't just feel sad, I felt unanchored. I felt alone in a way that even I struggled to put into words. The kind of alone where you can be surrounded by people and still feel like no-one sees you. The grief of my parents, the pain of *Baltic Folk* almost falling apart and the old wounds of infertility collided in a wave I wasn't ready for.

It was worse than the initial depression I had felt years ago when I lost the dream of motherhood because now I knew what grief could do. I knew I had to somehow survive it again.

This time I didn't collapse but I did slow down. I gave myself permission to be still. To cry. To do less. I turned inward and returned to the practices that had held me before: kinesiology, tapping, energy work, counselling, breathwork. These weren't luxuries, they were lifelines. They helped me make sense of emotions that had no words. They held me when I couldn't hold myself.

And slowly, like the seasons, something shifted.

We found a way forward for *Baltic Folk*. It didn't look like the original plan, but it didn't need to. We created a beautiful line of acrylic jewellery – bright, joyful, healing in its own right – while we searched for a new manufacturer who could bring our silver pieces to life. Eventually, we found one. In doing so, I realised that this journey of creation, loss and rebirth wasn't just about jewellery; it was about *me*.

I had learned that healing isn't linear. That grief can live in your bones and still sit beside joy. That starting over doesn't always feel brave; it often feels exhausting and vulnerable and full of doubt. I also knew that every time I thought the story was ending, something new was being born.

I used to think healing had a finish line. That if I did enough work, cleared enough blocks and learned enough tools, I would arrive at a place where I felt whole again. The truth is that healing is less like a staircase and more like a spiral. You circle back to the same wounds but from a different place each time. Sometimes you feel strong, other times you feel cracked wide open. Each time, you see a little more. You understand a little deeper. And the pain begins to transform into something useful.

I had reached a point where I could hold space for others from a grounded place, without giving myself away. I learned how to recognise when I was overextending, when I was rescuing instead of supporting and when I needed to pause instead of push. My practice matured because I matured. My sessions became gentler, deeper, more intuitive and more empowering. I was less about doing and more about *being with*.

Even as I grew into that version of myself, however, something still felt just slightly out of place. It was like I had all the pieces but not the map. I had done so much inner work – kinesiology, counselling, hypnotherapy, tapping, energy healing. All of it had helped me survive and evolve, yet something inside me was still craving a deeper understanding of how I was wired to operate and how to work *with* myself instead of constantly managing or fixing myself.

That's when I was introduced to Human Design life coaching. At first it was just a curiosity, but the more I explored, the more it resonated. It was like someone had written a blueprint of my soul and handed it to me with love. Human Design is a powerful tool that helps you remember who you were *born* to be before the world told you who you *should* be. It's a system that combines ancient wisdom with modern science to reveal how your energy works, how you're wired to make decisions and what alignment truly feels like for *you*. It didn't tell me anything I hadn't felt before but it gave language to what I already knew in my bones. It validated why certain things had always felt so hard and why others came so naturally. It reminded me that I wasn't broken; I just hadn't been living in alignment with how I was actually designed to move through the world.

Human Design became the final piece that pulled everything together. It helped me understand how to make decisions that felt right. It gave me permission to honour my energy and rhythm. It showed me why I'd burned out in the past and how to prevent it moving forward. It helped me trust myself more deeply than ever before.

And it brought me back to my centre, not the centre the world had told me I should live from but the one I had known all along. The one I had lost in grief and pain and over-giving – but never truly abandoned.

From that place, everything began to feel clearer. My work. My relationships. Even my boundaries. I started making decisions that felt peaceful instead of pressured. I stopped chasing and started allowing. I began creating again, not from desperation but from joy. I started dreaming about the next version of my business – not as a hustle but as a spacious, soul-led offering that could reach people without me needing to be everywhere at once.

I knew I wanted to take my work online. I wanted to guide others through their own return to self by using all the tools I had lived and learned. This time, it wasn't about proving anything. It was about sharing what had truly helped me come home to who I am.

Looking back now, I can see the through-line that connects it all. The child who felt she didn't belong. The woman whose body betrayed her. The grief that took everything she thought life would be. The losses that kept coming. And the quiet, stubborn, beautiful part of me that kept rising, again and again – not perfectly but faithfully.

There is no Plan A anymore and I've stopped searching for one. What I've come to understand is that life is not meant to be controlled; it's meant to be lived, responded to and danced with.

The plan I never saw coming – the one I never imagined for myself – has turned out to be the one that aligns most with who I really am.

I used to think my story was one of loss, and in many ways it is. I've lost the dream of motherhood. I've lost businesses, money, safety nets and people I love more than words can hold. I've lost roles and identities, future plans and familiar rhythms. I've walked through grief that silenced me and pain that left me breathless.

What I've come to realise is that underneath all that loss I also found myself.

I found strength I didn't know I had. I found stillness in the places I used to fill with noise. I found meaning – not in spite of the breakdowns but *because* of them. And I found a kind of quiet power that comes only from living every part of your truth.

This life I live now is not the one I planned. It's not Plan A. Or B. Or even C. But it is *mine* – and for the first time, it feels aligned.

If you are reading this in the middle of your own unravelling, if you're grieving something that no-one else seems to see, or feeling lost inside a life you didn't choose, please know this: you are not broken. You are being rewritten.

Let go of the pressure to go back to who you were because you're not meant to. You're meant to become someone new. Someone even more *you* than you've ever been.

You don't need a perfect plan. You need a pause. A breath. A beginning. Sometimes, the life you never expected becomes the one that fits you best. Sometimes, the plan you never saw coming turns out to be the one that brings you home – a new blueprint for your life.

If any part of my story has resonated with you, please know you don't have to walk your path alone. As a multi-award-winning, qualified life coach and multi-disciplinary wholistic health practitioner with lived experience, I offer a safe, compassionate space for you to explore your healing, reconnect with your truth and rebuild in alignment with who you truly are.

Anne Barratt *is a multi-award-winning holistic health practitioner with over twenty years of experience and the founder of* Empowering Health, *where she's spent the past decade helping women transform every area of their lives – from physical wellbeing to emotional healing, financial abundance, relationships and spiritual connection. With a long list of qualifications in complementary health, including kinesiology and quantum frequency technology, Anne blends evidence-based techniques with intuitive wisdom to create real, lasting change. She speaks from lived experience, having overcome her own health challenges, career reinvention and personal losses using the very methods she now teaches. Her corporate marketing background adds a practical edge to her deep, compassionate work. Anne is living proof that it's never too late to rewrite your story, reclaim your energy and realign with your purpose – on your terms.*

How I Lived With ADHD - and How I Would've Lived if I'd Known It

Michal Gabriel

When I was diagnosed last year, at the age of fifty-two, nothing changed – and everything changed. I often ask myself how I guided so many teenagers – who failed at school – to do their HSC and go to Uni … yet still feel like I failed as a mum? I knew what to do and I'm damn good at it too. So why couldn't I do it with my boys? Why not with my relationship? Why not with me?

The Hair Clip

I remember, at the age of five, getting ready for a function. Absorbing the excitement in the house, I went and put a hair clip on the front of my hairline, so everyone could see how beautiful it was. It made sense, no?

Apparently, only I could see the beauty in it. When Mum came to check on me, she saw it and said, "It doesn't look nice there. Why won't you try to stick it on the side?" She was so rude! She took it and gently gathered some hair on the right and placed the hair clip nicely at an angle.

Pfft! What did she know? She was only a fashion designer, and the hottest woman you've ever seen!

I said, "No! I like it here!" I pointed to the front and pulled the hair clip off my hair. It hurt and of course was followed by the automatic response of gathering my tight and young skin on my forehead to a frown and then allowing the tears.

I remember this moment because Mum kneeled to look me in the eyes and said, "You know Michali, you will meet a lot of people in your life, but you know, as your mum, I will always, always be totally honest with you and will always want the best for you. So when I suggested to change the hair clip, it is because you look even more beautiful like this."

After this, we were all ready. And me? Off I went to continue my life listening to everything my mum said, because she only wanted the best for me! The other thing this memory did was bring awareness of how much I can influence my boys without knowing. Mum doesn't remember this moment at all.

I wanted to do everything to give my boys the best of my knowledge. The more they know, the better their lives will be. That's what I believed – and still do. Over the years, I had such great ideas for everything! I'm the master of the greatest ideas. Truly. The problem is they were ideas. At best, we tried them for a week. Some even lasted three weeks! And then they were ... poof... gone.

If only I stuck to one thing. At least to the one I knew would've made the most impact on my relationship with my husband and boys.

He Doesn't Need Help. You Do!

Last year, I was diagnosed with ADHD and being on the autism spectrum.

The spectrum was a bit of a surprise, though it made sense of why, throughout my life, I'd craved connection but was the worst at facilitating and maintaining it. It's easy for people to say 'just call' or 'just message' but that's a big deal for someone on the spectrum.

Awareness is power. Now that I'm fifty-two I can do whatever I want.

The ADHD was obvious. My son – who is now eighteen – was diagnosed when he was in preschool. Well, not officially as I wasn't that quick to get it. I was a bit slow to see things – like when we (I) realised my eldest boy needed glasses. He was in Year 6 and when he wore his glasses for the first time, we walked down the street and he pointed to a tree and said, "Wow! How cool! The tree has patterns. It's got grooves in it." Fuck me! How long had he needed glasses, and I hadn't known?

With my youngest – the one with ADHD – I was told he needed some help. Told in the 'gentle way' teachers use. The way that, if you can read between the lines, really means, 'your kid is fucked and needs to be medicated because he cannot learn like this and the class cannot learn like this.'

Being a coordinator for educational projects thirty years ago – way before society knew that it's how we program our kids – I 'knew' that it's not the kid, it's the teacher. So, at the time, in my own way – the way a parent with no confidence says, 'He doesn't need help. You do!'

– I could've also added, "I know it's you! And there's nothing you can do because this is the system you're in. You're both fucked."

Essentially, what I'm saying here is that I blamed all the teachers. I said they were lazy. I said that all they wanted were zombies in the room so it would be nice and quiet for them to tick the curriculum boxes.

And I did say just that, in the same gentle way I'd been told my son needed 'help'.

I said, "You know when I get the best out of him? When I talk to him, and when I give him micro successes. Like when I teach him that one plus one equals two, at the end of the day, I'll give him a test about 'one plus one' and not ask him what 'two plus one' is. Maybe you could get the best out of him if you changed the way you approached things and actually talk to him." (This is true, by the way, but it's not the way the school system is built. Again, another story.)

It didn't work and I refused to medicate the kid. Year after year, I was literally hiding from the teachers at pick-up time. I listened to the heartbreaking stories describing how my son was going through the same things, following the same path, that I had. The way we both connected to kids no-one else socialised with. How we protected the ones that annoyed everyone. How we had the desire to be part of the cool group because we knew we belonged there – but no-one else knew it because they weren't mature enough to know. They didn't know we're all connected. And they didn't know that love is the answer. It was too big for them to know yet.

Stupid Story. What Was I Thinking?

It's probably the most stupid thing ever but let me share this with you so you'll understand the level and process of thinking someone with an

ADHD brain goes through. Then you'll see how serious I was about making other people feel good about themselves.

I was about ten. Back then, we literally used to walk down the street just for the sake of going out. Whenever I saw an old person or a couple walking slowly when I was walking down the street, I used to walk past them really fast. If they had a stick, they received 'extra points' from me – they were worth more in the 'poor old people world' I'd created! Anyway, I walked quickly to get past them just so I could then walk more slowly in front of them.

I'll say it again: I used to walk fast to pass them, just so I could then walk slower in front of them.

The aim of the game was to make them feel good about themselves. In this scenario, in my head, they would see that sometimes young kids can also be slow walkers. That way, they wouldn't feel sad or alone; there are others in the world, young and old.

How can you un-fuck that?

Stupidity or not, I did it – true story. It's definitely a Paulina scenario – a hard-core people-pleaser.

I developed my people-pleasing when I was a bit younger with my mum when she was upset about something. All I wanted to do was please my mum. I practised it so much that it became my second nature.

Tell Me Who Your Friends Are, and I'll Tell You Who You Are

Dad always said, "Tell me who your friends are and I'll tell you who you are."

I just wanted to please everyone and make everyone happy – especially if someone was sitting by themselves or being treated badly by others. So, because of this, I got in trouble from my teachers and from my parents for hanging out with them. I was also rejected by my classmates as I was going with the 'unpopular' kids.

I remember sitting with the tallest girl in class – everyone called her 'Giraffe'. She crossed her feet inwards – and down came the 'class queen' who laughed at her inward feet. Then she had her 'followers'. Then the whole class was behind the queen. I stood in front of them all, with the Giraffe behind me, fighting her fight. I was telling everyone off and telling the queen, "How dare you do it. How dare you bring the whole class to do it to her!" I was in Year 5 – and for about a month, no-one talked to me. No-one showed up to my birthday.

It's funny (not) how my youngest boy went through the same. He was a bit more 'on it' with the eldest people but never to this degree. He clearly remembers a story that affected all his primary school years. He'd protected one of the kids because a girl was treating him badly. While protecting this child, he pushed the girl because she was in his face. The whole class chased him and blamed him. They probably still remember it, even now.

My Heart Was Shattered

Finally, when he was in Year 5, I got him diagnosed. It was a high positive of both ADHDs. I tried natural ways – changed his diet, filled him vitamins and so on. Then, at the end of Year 5, I gave him the medication – Ritalin – just for half a day to try it.

He came home after school, old enough to know how he feels and how to talk, and he said, "Mum! Why didn't you give me this medication before?" Then he told me he'd just had the best day at school ever!

My heart was shattered.

I'd wrecked his life. All his primary school years could've looked better. He could've had friends. He could've had fun going to school.

What had I done?

It's okay to fuck up my life, but my boys? He was the youngest, so what if my older boys had it too? How could I have been so blind to all of it?

My middle boy was very popular everywhere he went. When he went to high school, he was accepted to an art class. The poor boy was there for three years. He was not good at art, yet he was in a class full of artistic personalities. These were the worst years of his life! He had to go and see a psychologist for depression. How could I not see it before? When it clicked, I wrote to the school: how the fuck did you let it go for so long? His teachers were in the class and saw it. Sure, art can be in the eye of the person ... blah blah, blah ... but for fuck's sake! This was a recipe for creating self-doubt and low self-esteem.

I'll admit I was stupid not to realise it sooner. But the teachers ... they were with him in class. Couldn't they have said something?

Maybe, if I were more aware and had paid more attention, my boys' lives would've been different. My life would've been different. My relationships would've been different.

But they weren't. And I wasn't. And that's the thing.

After doing inner-child work, I realised it doesn't matter how we raised our kids, how we lived or what we said and did. Today, my boys are eighteen, twenty-two and twenty-three. I'm fifty-two and my husband is nearly fifty-three. Today, we're old enough to know better. Today, we can choose to remember how fucked up it was. I can choose to wish I did it better.

Whatever I did or didn't do – it shaped those boys to be who they are today. I'm so proud of them as they all have beautiful hearts. They're all well-mannered and know they can choose their future.

Today, we all know that no matter what our parents said and did, they did what they knew and they did it with good intention.

When I Learned to Say, 'Fuck It!'

Just before I went to high school, I said 'fuck it' for the first time. It was nothing special, no-one even knew it was my turning point. It was over something simple, when my friends said let's go somewhere after my parents said no. And when I said it – it felt good! 'Fuck it' made me feel so good to be bad that I didn't want to be good ever again! It was like unleashing the real me. I will not give a fuck anymore about saying what I have to say.

I started my own fashion style – inspired by my mum. I was the first one to create rips in the uniform shirt. I remember all the girls bringing their shirts for me to do it for them. Since we all had to be unique, I did it in different ways for each girl. It was so cool!

At fifteen, I pierced my nose and hung out with the punk and goth kids. I loved it. We all said 'Fuck it' – a lot. I liked how we looked. I liked how none of us cared. Finally, I could feel comfortable looking different. I insisted on being unique. When someone in the group pierced their nose like me, I went to get a second nose piercing. When someone had the second one, I went and got my third. No-one had a big nose like mine – big enough to fit three – so I won.

Then I Was a Mum

Finally, I got my motorbike licence and was free to go wherever. Mostly, I liked to feel the freedom when the wind touched my face.

Whatever I did, I always kept my unique self and my 'Fuck it' attitude.

I took it with me when I joined the army. I joined a group that did the army together as a commune. It was one of the best experiences in my life.

I took it with me when I went to university.

I took it when I was a tutor, a teacher and the coordinator for educational projects. I took it when I lived in the kibbutz. When I got married. When I moved to Australia.

And then, I was a mum.

When the boys came, I lost it. I lost myself. I was no longer the young woman Barry married. I was serious. I took life very seriously and concentrated a lot on the boys. I concentrated on work, growth, friends and our relationship. It was like being asleep for twenty-five years.

I've been taking my medications for about four months now – at the time of writing this. Even though it's been more than a year since I was diagnosed, I didn't think I would need the medication. I said, "I've learned how to live with it. I'm in my fifties and have managed so far, so why now?"

But then, when I did finally take it, just like my son had before me, I said, "Why didn't I take it before?"

Today

Today, I'm aware.

Today, I know it's my choice. I can either choose the easy way and continue with my habits – or I can choose the hard way, rebuild who I want to be and decide what the rest of my story will be.

Michal Gabriel is a global and national award-winning salon owner, natural brow specialist, educator, and mum of three. For over twenty years in the beauty industry, she helped women turn cringe into a smile when they look in the mirror. Diagnosed with ADHD and being on the spectrum early last year, Michal shares how she lived and is living with ADHD and loving life. Her goal is to show women that awareness is important and that we all have the choice to decide how to live life.

Loss, Grief and Survival

Despair

Shaz Cini

Despair can be hard to describe, but mostly, it's that feeling that everything in your life is imploding. Deep loss, grief, anger and frustration all rolling around in your head. Emptiness, nothingness and an even deeper desire to just give up and quit it all. You can't seem to find a way out.

You may wonder whether life is even worth living if all that happens is loss, great loss and that soul-deep feeling of hopelessness. The pain that you don't want to face or go through again. There is a way through despair, but you first need to believe that there is something better just around the corner.

Many years ago, I suffered what I thought was a catastrophic loss. In a single weekend, I miscarried my twins, the house I lived in was sold and I needed to find a new place to live and, on top of that, my car (which ended up being written off) was badly damaged in a freak hailstorm that swept through my town.

Blessedly, I had a great support network who helped me find a place to live before Christmas and, perhaps because of this, I felt like I needed to be strong and couldn't lose my mind or grieve the loss of my babies. I had fight on and look for a new house as I had two other people living with me and they were counting on me too. That motivation kept me moving forward.

Life continued as it had before and I began to recover and live again. Or so I thought.

A deep pain festered within me. Sadness was never really far away, but I thought I had no choice but to continue on.

Over the next few years, my health deteriorated, and one thing after another led to me nearly dying from complications four times in six months. Although the despair I was feeling was unimaginable, there was this small glimmer that I continued to hold onto – one day things would be different.

Even though those things brought me down, a dream still existed inside of me.

Something that told me there was more to life than this. Life was not meant to be about suffering; it was to live with joy, and have a purpose and a passion within yourself to go and do what you love. Those thoughts still existed within, but I didn't quite know how to tap into them. Deep down, though, I always believed something better was just around the corner. Hanging on to that belief – that spark of hope – led me to start my crystal business.

There was a calling inside my heart to share crystals, healing and spirituality with the world; however, with not a lot of money to invest, I did it the hard way. I started with nothing but love and joy on my side, and a passion within that knew no limits. I began sharing my knowledge with people, developed amazing connections and delivered messages that people needed to hear.

They say when you're passionate about something, you never work a day in your life. That's exactly what this was for me. I loved the work I did. Spreading messages to people always brought joy to my heart. I often worked over sixteen hours a day building my business, learning new skills and coming up with different ideas to make it grow. I upgraded myself and my skills in many ways – and I thrived throughout it all.

Even after leaving my first business location, I still wanted to make it work, so I pivoted and took the business home. I was still very passionate about helping others and this was a minor fork in the road, so to speak. I had all these big ideas and plans that swirled in my head. I started doing events on the road. I expanded my network. Eventually, I went into partnership with someone to grow my business and open a shop.

Things were great for a few months, and then it started to fall apart. The shop was okay but the partnership was not. In the end, it dissolved. My love for crystals and this business had me convincing myself that I wasn't worried. I thought everything would be okay because I believed I could sort it out. I believed it would still succeed. I tried – but I wasn't able to make it all work.

Now, for the second time in my life, I'd lost everything.

And I mean everything.

I'd lost the one thing in my life that had any meaning. I'd lost my business while I was at a funeral for my aunt, a week after my uncle died. I'd lost my home. I had nowhere to go. I had no income. I was going to lose my car because it was tied to my business. I was trying to come to terms with betrayal.

It was a very dark time and the despair was unbearable.

Was I a failure?

I'd trusted people, and they'd done me wrong. That trust had cost me something I'd worked my arse off to build. Something I'd created from nothing.

Worst of all, I'd lost myself along the way.

You know that feeling you get when you're doing what you're meant to be doing? I loved my business. I'd spent years building it up and doing the work I loved. I truly believed I was doing what I was meant to be doing.

When it all fell apart, I was rudderless. I felt helpless and I was in pain. I couldn't think. I didn't know what to do and I couldn't face starting over again from scratch. The first time I lost everything was worse but I'd had friends and family there to support me. This time, I had no-one. My aunt, who would usually have helped me, was older and sick. She had her own problems to face and deal with. She'd lost her beloved sister and as much as I wanted to be there for her, because of my own struggles, I couldn't be.

I'd lost who I was. My whole identity. I was doing what I loved and I'd invested five years into it. There wasn't anything of me outside of my crystal shop. I didn't know who I was. I didn't know what I wanted in life. All I knew was that I didn't really want to be here at all.

I'd been fighting for my whole life and I just didn't want to do it anymore.

The thoughts and feelings inside of me were so low that, at the time, I wasn't sure I'd survive it all. I just didn't have the strength or the desire to start again.

What did I have to live for, really?

No partner. No kids. My favourite person in the world was ill and possibly dying. My business – the thing I lived for – had been taken away from me.

What was the point of it all?

Why be here at all when there was nothing good in my life anymore? I couldn't fight the voices that kept telling me I was worthless. I didn't deserve anything. The voice told me that I shouldn't be surprised that all of this had happened. Wasn't this exactly what I'd expected? Didn't I know anything good would be taken away from me? Surely I realised I was nobody.

I'd lost the desire to fight. I couldn't take it anymore and the only thoughts in my head were of vengeance and harm.

When it all got too much, and I knew I was going to do something that would hurt myself and others, I sat outside the mental hospital in Penrith crying and fighting with my conscience as to whether to go inside and talk to someone or go and get the vengeance I wanted. The devil inside me was strong that day – I was alternating between what I knew was right and wanting to hurt the person who'd hurt me. The person who kept hurting me.

The thing is, I was being cyber-bullied – by text. I was being baited. Even though I was normally a strong person and didn't usually accept this sort of behaviour, I had no strength left to fight against it. I'd been fighting for a resolution to what had happened and had been trying to get help so I could retrieve what had been taken from me. However, I also knew that sometimes you just have to walk away from a fight you are unable to win.

That was where I was at – walking away or taking vengeance.

The only problem was that I had nowhere to go and no way to get there. I was at the lowest of lows – hence, my fight outside the hospital. I wanted to end it all and the choice I was debating was whether to go out alone or take a bunch of people with me.

It wasn't what I wanted to do, but I felt the mental hospital was the safest place for me. The feelings inside me – the anger and pain – were out of control. It scared me because I knew that I had a temper and I knew that when I lost it bad, consequences happen. So, when a nurse came out to check on me, I told her about this fight and we decided I needed to be admitted for a while.

In the end, the hospital was not that helpful. Even though they said they would help me, I couldn't get any assistance. They kicked me out after a few days as I was internalising my problems – and I still had the common sense to differentiate between right and wrong.

I was discharged and sent to a women's hostel for a week. After a bad episode in there with another women who stole medication that I didn't want to take anyway, I left. A friend had offered me a place to stay, so I packed all my stuff and moved up to Maitland for a while.

Moving away was a little bit like out of sight, out of mind; if I was far enough away from the people and place that hurt me, it couldn't hurt so much. Healing started to take place and, after a few weeks of sleep and solitude, I started to venture out a little. On my birthday, I had a spiritual visit from Archangel Michael. He told me I was strong and I'd get through this, but there was still work for me to do.

I was not happy, to say the least. I yelled and screamed, "I am not strong. I don't want to be strong." I refused to start again and I screamed at Archangel Michael, "STOP telling me I AM STRONG!"

He smiled at me.

"The next person you get to tell me I'm strong ... I'm going to hit them," I yelled.

A week or two later, my friend was hosting an art class at the Newcastle Spiritual Church. Before the church service, she was holding an art lesson in which she was teaching people to connect with and draw the Archangels. She asked me to go with her.

Still mad at the world, I really didn't want to go, but with a little cajoling from her, I agreed to go. After all, I loved art (even though I'm not very good at it) and wanted to learn more about drawing angels.

The day started out well. It was a small class and we were paired off to do an angel drawing for each other with a message.

I don't remember the angel I drew for my partner, but I do remember who she drew for me and what she said. It's burned into my memory – the Archangel Michael. And his message? You are strong and will get through this.

As you might imagine, I was not happy at all. In fact, I was pissed off. I could see Archangel Michael standing right next to my partner as she said it – and he was smiling at me. I felt like he was laughing at me, so I told him he was a f*ing c*.

My partner, as you can imagine, was shocked as hell – I was in a church and swearing at an Archangel. I told her why I said that to him, and how I'd sworn if he sent one more person to tell me I was strong, I was going to punch them in the face.

She smiled at me, laid a hand on my arm and said, "You won't hit me, dear. You're much too kind for that – and you *are* strong. I know you will come back better than before, and you will succeed." She then leaned over and gave me a hug. I cried in her arms and told her I couldn't do it anymore. She just smiled and nodded and said, "Yes, you will."

After the art class, we stayed for the church service. The medium was up on the podium sharing a story about how to beat anxiety and how if you play rhythms on your chest or body, their patterns interrupt your system to get you out of your breakdown. She also talked about the neuroscience behind it, the reasons it was effective and what happened from a psychological point of view.

I'd never heard about any of this but, as I sat there, I realised I'd been doing this for myself for a long time already. That exact thing got me out of a deep panic attack when I was in shock. And now, understanding what I'd done seemed to shift something inside me.

Archangel Michael came back and sat next to me. "See how much you know already?" he said. "See how strong you are? You do these things unconsciously without knowing why but trusting it will work. It has saved you and the other people you've already shared it with."

Then he told me I'd come back to do my spiritual work – but it had to change. I had to focus on emotional healing, mindset and the way you think and see yourself. He told me I already had a lot of knowledge and skills in this area, but that he'd share more with me. He wanted me to listen, have an open mind and allow my healing to take place.

The medium came to me with a message that day too. She told me that what I'd been through had ended; that I was on the rise again.

I was more open to this.

She looked straight into my eyes and said, "You have to share your knowledge with people. You will have a bigger audience than you had before. Most of it will be online and you'll work with people around the world."

I couldn't see it and didn't really understand it – but I kept an open mind. Archangel Michael told me he'd help me and I just had to allow the flow.

We went home that day and, once again, I had a spark of hope. This was something to take my mind off my own problems and a new idea to focus on. I started to look at Facebook again. I reconnected with some people and did some free courses. Videos about mindset, healing and overcoming obstacles showed up in my news feed. Inspirational stories and how to rise up again were right in front of me. I also happened to belong to a Facebook group where we could trade services with each other.

I wasn't sure I wanted to do readings again – I was still sort of mad – but a lady was offering some emotional healing and kinesiology services, and I wanted to see if that would help me. I was ready to release some of the baggage I'd been carrying and knew I needed help with this.

I organised a trade. During my healing session, the lady mentioned something that really hit home. We cleared something deep that really set me on my healing path.

A few days later, another video popped up online. It was from lady called Lisa Nicholls. I'd never heard of her but her story hit home for me. At one point, she said, "You are your own rescue." This was like a sledgehammer to my solar plexus.

No-one was coming to save me; I have to do it myself.

That night, I had another encounter with Archangel Michael. We talked about Lisa and her story and how much it hit home. "See," he said, "that's really what you're meant to be doing. Helping other people heal, see the best of themselves and let go of their pasts so they can create beautiful futures."

When I asked him how to do that, he said, "Manifest it."

I didn't know a lot about manifesting at the time. I'd heard of it but didn't know a lot, but new courses and people talking about it somehow showed up on my Facebook the next day.

Along with dozens of coaches, motivational speakers, healers and others, I was inundated with positivity. I binge-watched videos and courses on healing, coaching manifesting and spiritual development. I learned. I committed. I grew and changed. And, slowly, I started to live again.

I was gaining so much new knowledge and, being someone who likes to test and measure things, I had to share it with others. I wasn't in a completely good headspace, but I was on the way to recovery.

Archangel Michael told me there are lots of other people out there who don't know about this stuff either. He challenged me – bullied me – to share it with others. He literally dared me to offer it to others, so we started negotiating terms. I told him I would do it as long as I had five people willing to learn and, since I was already doing a manifesting challenge in which I'd set a goal of $1000 in twenty-one days, I knew it had to cost $150. I told him I'd do it if I got the numbers – and only then.

The bastard got to work.

I shared a post saying I'd teach a 30-day program – *Awaken Your Inner Goddess*. I had five women join within thirty minutes of posting it. So – when I tell you that your soul or Archangels want you to do something and to trust they'll make it happen, I mean it.

I didn't really want to do it – but I knew I had to. I had to create everything on the go. We had heaps of fun, the girls loved it and I gained a lot from it as well. I tested heaps of manifesting techniques and mindset shifts. I healed my inner child. I discovered and aligned my shadow. And, most of all, I found my identity again. I found myself.

I'd found a new purpose – a new passion. This lit a massive spark inside me; one of learning and loving life again.

Even when I had a falling out with my friend and had to move out quickly – and even though I had nowhere to go – I was fine. I was fired up and knew that things would work out for me. I trusted my higher self when it said things would work out.

Why?

Because I'd surrendered to my higher self. I'd told my soul, "You direct me, I'll listen and follow. Even when I'm afraid, even when I can't see the outcome for myself, I'll follow your signs and guidance."

I'd started to trust in the Universe and believe in myself.

I went to stay with a friend for a few weeks, finding peace and solace there. I talked to another friend, and he invited me to move in with him and his family in Rockhampton. So I bought a one-way ticket, packed what I could and what I needed – basically just some clothes and my laptop – and I boarded a plane off to a new adventure.

I was still lost.

I still felt a little soulless and worthless – but I had that spark of hope. That's what I called it back then, not realising it was pure faith in God and myself.

I hopped on a plane to Rockhampton and my friend, Corey, picked me up. He was excited to see me and I was happy to be up there. I was away from all the energy of my pain, and I was excited about the things I was learning and where I could take my life. I didn't have a clear picture yet, but I had some ideas.

Funnily enough, when we got to Corey's house, his mum said, "How long are you visiting for?"

Eyes wide, I turned around to Corey and asked what was going on. "Didn't you tell her?" I said.

"Tell me what?" she said.

Casually, Corey said, "Oh yeah, Mum, I told Shaz she could move in with us."

I was mortified. I was scared and frozen. I had no idea she didn't know his plans. It was so like Corey not to worry about those kinds of things.

Ramona (Corey's mum) invited me to sit with her. We chatted and got to know each other better. Then she said she wasn't sure what would happen, but we'd work it out and I'd be okay there. We got on like a house on fire. Zoe (Corey's sister) had to go away to work, so I had her room for a time. I started to heal and recover. Rockhampton is where I found myself again.

Corey's family became my family. I still consider them family today. I didn't stay up there long – only three months – but during that time I had an office set up so I could invest in my healing journey, learn new things, offer some client services and put together things to rebuild my life.

I started to dream again. I started to consider what I wanted out of life. I started to live. I worked hard, spending a lot of time at my computer each day. I shifted my mindset, healed my trauma, let go of my past and found my freedom again. I started to smile and laugh.

I'd found happiness.

After thinking I was lost, I'd found my place in the world again. Well, the beginning of it, anyway.

I studied different types of coaching and learned from some amazing speakers, putting all their suggestions into practice. I shifted the way I saw myself. I started to reconnect with people who'd previously supported me – and I shared what I was learning. It was all fascinating. I'd thought most people would know about the things I was sharing – but they didn't and suddenly I was helping people who needed help.

I meditated daily. I reconnected with my soul, surrendering everything to it and telling it to show me what to do each day. I read spiritual books, followed all the rituals, journalled it all out and cleared my thoughts. All this time, I was learning new skills. Ho'oponopono – the ancient Hawaiian practice of forgiveness – was a huge game-changer for me. This practice helped me forgive myself, let go of my past and thank the Universe for its support. It taught me more about myself and how to accept the love of self.

I'd already been on a self-love journey. Through all the darkness, I never really lost it like I'd lost it before. I fell in love with who I was and who I was becoming. I chose my new identity. It was deep work. There was lots of crying at night, lots of releasing when I was able and lots of awareness of self.

I became conscious. I became present. I communicated with God every day and talked to my higher self. Each day, I'd ask: "How can

I be of service?" and "What is this teaching me?" These questions became my mantras. They became my purpose in moving forward. I held myself accountable and I showed up for myself.

Then, when I was able, I showed up for other people.

I'd found my strength again and rediscovered my true talent.

Ever since I was a child, I'd always wanted to be a teacher. I discovered coaching was my version of teaching. I learned that I was a spiritual teacher of the soul and of understanding your soul's mission in this world. We all have one. It's that reason for living. The purpose we come down to fulfil. My goal is to help people remember what that purpose is and to set you on a path to achieve all you want along your journey.

My belief is that if I can spark the light of purpose in you, then you can spark the light in someone else and, together, we can heal and light up the world. The world is a much better place when we're all living our true purpose. We live happily and freely, and we create miracles. That's what life is all about.

In hindsight, I can see that despair was not the end of my story but the doorway to a new beginning. What once felt like complete emptiness has now become a life filled with meaning and purpose.

I love who I am.

I love the life I am living.

Most of all, I show up exactly as I am.

This journey helped me find myself. Those losses helped me open my heart to the path I walk today. They made me into exactly who I am and I love myself. I couldn't have become who I am without what I went through – they are all facets of myself.

What was once a spark of hope now burns brightly as a fire in my soul that guides me every single day. I nurture that fire and show up – for me and for the world I'm creating around myself.

The big thing this journey has taught me is that despair does not last forever. Even in your darkest moments, there's always a glimmer of light we call hope and that belongs to our soul. There's always a light waiting for us at the end of the tunnel – something brighter, deeper and more aligned with who we truly are.

Follow that light.

Shaz Cini *is a transformational life coach and psychic medium. She is the creator of* Shine with Shaz *– her signature coaching program that helps women heal emotional wounds, reclaim their power and align with their true selves. Known for her no-fluff, deeply compassionate approach, Shaz blends neuro-linguistic programming (NLP), hypnosis and intuitive guidance to help her clients build unshakable confidence and create a life they love. Her work is grounded in the belief that we are souls having a human experience and that everything we need is already within us. Through her podcast,* Spiritual Awakening with Shaz, *and her coaching programs, Shaz inspires women worldwide to step out of fear, embrace their worth and shine unapologetically.*

Life in Moments

SHEREE TIVENDALE

My journey as a civil celebrant is my life's purpose.

People often ask me what it's like being a celebrant and, to be honest, it's hard to sum it up neatly because it's not just a job – it's a life. A life made up of small but powerful moments, shared with others. Moments of love, loss, hope, celebration and, sometimes, heartbreak. It's a privilege and a huge honour – and it's something I never ever take for granted.

It started when I was little. I didn't play shops or schools like other kids – I played weddings. I'd marry my dolls, play dress-ups in my mum's wedding dress, pick bouquets from our farm garden and give little speeches to the attending toys and pets on the front steps of our family farmhouse. I'd also play weddings with my friends in primary school. Even back then, I suppose something in me understood the magic of ceremony and the meaning that lives inside words, symbols and small rituals. I've always loved people's stories. I love hearing them. I love sharing them. And I've always wanted to honour them.

I'm blessed to be able to do what I love – working across weddings, funerals, memorials, naming days and all life celebrations. I'm also a Reiki Master and continuing my lifelong studies. I think I'll probably always be studying something as I love learning and growing.

I pour everything I've got into each ceremony because I know how important these moments are to people. They're milestones, markers and memories in the making. To be invited into those moments is an honour beyond words.

I grew up in the 1980s when there was a quiet undercurrent of change happening for women. We were told we could 'have it all' – careers, families, perfect homes, balanced lives. But what that actually meant was we were suddenly expected to do it all. To be everything to everyone and do it with a smile.

That pressure still lingers. I'm a mum, a daughter, a friend and a businesswoman. I juggle ceremonies with family commitments. I've written many ceremonies in the car. In fact, sometimes I feel like I spend more time in the car than anywhere else because I travel all over the state for services. It can certainly feel like juggling. Some days, I'm better at juggling than others. There can be very late nights and very early mornings to make it all work. I've come to see it as part of the enriched work that I do because, through it all, I've found a way to love what I do every day and that feels deeply meaningful to me.

I've made some really hard choices in my life – the kind that don't come without grief, even when they come from a place of strength.

When I was sixteen, I fell pregnant. I made the decision not to become a mother at that time. It was the right decision for who I was then – but that doesn't mean it was easy. There's a little place in my heart where that grief still lives. I carry that experience with me and I think it's shaped how I honour the hard roads that others walk. I often think of who that child might have been. That kind of decision never really leaves you.

Years later, I married young and quickly – and it ended just as fast. Six weeks in, I discovered betrayal and made the decision to walk away. Some people said I was brave; some said I was reckless. I say I did what was necessary. I've learned to trust myself, even when others don't understand the path I take.

My second marriage was longer. I become a stepmother and that was such a wonderful time in my life. I was only twenty-three but I relished the time to relive childhood and zoo trips and kids parties and playing weddings again with dolls. As time progressed, the marriage gave me two of the greatest gifts of my life – my beautiful children, Charlotte and Alexander. In the end, our marriage didn't work. We tried – I feel like I gave it everything I could – but maybe it had never really worked in the first place. I don't regret it, though, because it led to me becoming a mum. For that, I'm endlessly grateful.

Then there was my third engagement – I don't think this one will ever make it down the aisle. A decade later, we just focus on our son, Teddy, who is an incredible blessing. So, while love has looked different in my own life, I consider myself lucky and joke that I'm the celebrant that isn't married. I have three children though – three beautiful souls I get to call my babies and that's everything to me. It also helps me deeply understand how people feel with first, second and beyond marriages and blended families.

No matter what the ending is, I still believe in love. I see it every day in the couples I marry, in the families I stand beside at funerals and in the new parents beaming at naming days. Love isn't always tidy or easy, but it is always worth celebrating.

Before I became a celebrant, I worked in marketing, event management, admin and human resources. Funnily enough, all those roles taught me something I use every day now.

From marketing, I learned how to tell stories that connect. From events, I learned how to juggle details, people, and logistics while keeping my cool. From admin, I learned to stay organised and anticipate needs. From HR, I learned how to listen – really listen – and hold space for people in their most vulnerable moments. It didn't feel like a direct path at the time but looking back, I can see it was all leading here. To this work. To this life.

At the moment, I'm studying counselling. It's giving me even deeper insight into people, grief, trauma and the human condition. It's helping me become an even better celebrant, listener and support person. I think learning keeps us curious. It reminds us that we're never finished. There's always more to understand and more to grow into. For me, that's exciting.

I also have some side passions, like building projects, which I find incredibly creative and satisfying. I enjoy craft projects too. One of my earliest memories of creativity was preparing exhibits for the Whittlesea Show. I have a competitive streak – although it's mostly with myself. I always want to do better. I want to make it better. When things don't go well, it really upsets me. I try so hard. I love to cook and bake, and I've made many platters for my couples over the years – especially in Covid lockdowns when that was all we could do to celebrate together. I also enjoy entertaining and having my friends and their children all come together. There's nothing quite like a table full of food and surrounded by laughter.

I'm really lucky to have a supportive network of celebrants and a supportive family. My mum still helps me by drying rose petals from her garden for ceremonies. My brother often collects things for me too, and my dad always listens to all my stories, I'm so grateful for all my family and my friends because they keep me grounded and loved in ways that words don't quite capture. I've made some wonderful celebrant friends. My greatest admiration is for my colleague and friend, Dally Messenger, the principal of the Internal College of Celebrants, who I now work with and who was always there, guiding me and mentoring me, in my early days as a celebrant. Dally is still only a call away, and he is a constant inspiration to me.

Covid really turned everything upside down for a while. I still have nightmares about home schooling while trying to reschedule weddings and funerals and reassure couples who were completely heartbroken. The lockdowns were devastating – the constant changes, the plans undone, the heartbreak for couples who'd dreamed of a certain date, a certain season, a certain moment. It was relentless and financially crushing.

Out of that chaos, however, came something life-changing.

My beautiful friend Kristy trusted me with something sacred; she asked me to write and lead her nana's funeral. I never thought I could do funerals because really I'm a softie, I cry watching the news. I'm such a crier if I'm not the celebrant at a wedding. But that moment changed the course of my life's work. Kristy believed in me and I found that I could hold it together when I needed to. That service shifted something in me. I realised I could do it and I loved it, what an honour.

Since then, I've written and led so many funerals; it has become one of the most meaningful parts of my work. One of the greatest honours in this work is being invited back into a family's life. In one beautiful family, I've been asked by three out of four siblings (so far) to officiate their weddings, and that honestly means the world to me. It's the kind of quiet compliment that says, we trust you with our most important days.

Equally touching was the time I met a family to lead their grandmother's funeral and, not long after, I was invited to officiate the granddaughter's wedding. My heart was full. To be part of both their grief and their celebration – that's what this work is all about. It's the honour of becoming a trusted presence across generations, across chapters, in both tears and joy.

I get to meet the most wonderful people and be there when they need support, guidance or just someone who truly sees them. Being able to help at a time of loss, and then again in a moment of love, is incredibly humbling. This work allows me to become a small but meaningful part of people's lives and I'm grateful for that every single day.

Some of the most special ceremonies I've been part of have taken me beyond my own backyard. Getting to lead a wedding in Bali was such a heartfelt and moving experience. Standing with them on the rooftop, bringing cultural elements together and the teary smiles all around – it was unforgettable. I'm forever grateful to Brooke and Amitoz for that moment in time. Emily and Leigh's wedding in Port Douglas was one where we all cried – the love was thick in the air and tissues were needed by everyone. The people, the setting, the love – it was one of those moments where you could just feel the magic.

However, two of the hardest moments were my greatest honour. Losing my two friends, Genevive and Tabitha, to cancer two weeks apart was heart-wrenching. It was two of the hardest days of my life, but I'm glad I could lead their services and tell their stories; to be asked to do that for them was a privilege. I'll never forget leading Tabitha's coffin out of the chapel. I cried the whole way out but I'm glad I was able to say everything for her and I think of them both every time I see a rainbow after a storm. It reminds me that life is still beautiful, even when it hurts. Those sorts of memories never fade.

I've travelled interstate many times, both for weddings and funerals. Each one holds its own special place in my heart. Whether it's a chapel in the country or a beachside ceremony far from home, it's an incredible privilege to be asked to go wherever I'm needed and I always will. I'll travel anywhere and everywhere because love and remembrance aren't bound by geography.

My heart is full doing what I love.

Sheree Tivendale *is a vibrant and dedicated civil celebrant, organiser and proud mum. Based in Broadford, Victoria, she has been creating and delivering ceremonies that matter for over fourteen years across her home state and beyond. From heartfelt weddings and vow renewals to meaningful funerals, memorials, naming days and other life celebrations, Sheree brings warmth, care and creativity to every occasion.*

With a professional background in marketing, human resources, community engagement and project management, Sheree brings a unique blend of organisation, empathy and insight to her work. These skills have helped her build a celebrant practice that is not only heartfelt and human-centred but also beautifully run behind the scenes.

Known for her calm presence, genuine connection and engaging delivery, Sheree specialises in ceremonies that are authentic, personal and truly memorable. Whether traditional or modern, intimate or grand, each service is carefully crafted to reflect the individuals at its heart.

As a mum Sheree understands the joy and chaos of everyday life and embraces both with humour and grace. As an event organiser, she is a juggler of many things from timelines, emotions, logistics, tissues and tender moments, with everything handled with care and precision.

Sheree believes in the power of ceremony to honour life's most meaningful chapters. It is her greatest privilege to walk alongside others as they celebrate love, honour legacy and mark the moments that matter most.

The Path Back to Pleasure

Jo Goddard

There's a moment that lives in my body as a quiet scream. It's the moment my body said *no*, but I didn't yet know how to listen.

My husband raped me – once. Yes, that's bad, but perhaps more haunting were the days and months after, where I kept letting him touch me even though I didn't want him to. Not because he was a monster – but because I was disempowered. I'd confused strength with sacrifice. I thought being a good wife meant going through the motions. I had no idea what true embodied consent felt like, let alone how to voice it.

This is a story about reclaiming pleasure after that experience. Not just pleasure in intimacy, but in myself. In my voice. My truth. My desires. It's about the slow, sacred unravelling that led me back to my body, back to my power and, ultimately, back to life.

The Good Wife

I married at twenty-six with good intentions. I was in love with the boy I'd grown up with for most of my life. The safe boy. The known boy. We'd been together since we were nineteen. He was a comfortable choice. It was right for that age and stage of my life.

I wanted partnership. A family. Belonging. I wanted the life we're sold in movies – the happy ending, the loyal heart, the certainty, the safety. And I believe I had that for a little while – before life became real, before we became parents with growing responsibilities, and before the stress of life pulled us apart and we didn't have the emotional maturity to sit in the discomfort together.

Then it became distant and resentful. It became emotionally empty. There was silence where communication should have been prioritised. Intimacy was either dormant or performed but not real. When he crossed my most scared body boundary and took his pleasure without my consent, something cracked. I didn't leave. I didn't scream. I didn't even cry.

Instead, I internalised it as *my* failure. I wondered if I'd led him on. Was my inability to say no – I was intoxicated and not fully conscious – my fault? Had I overlooked the truth of who this man really was?

When Strength Is Actually Suffering

Looking back, I see now that I made it mean something about my worth. I told myself I was broken, but I wasn't going to break my family. I decided my pleasure was irrelevant. I had a family with this man. I could pour myself into the story that he was a 'good man who'd made a bad decision' – and believe that this story would protect my family and my kids.

I doubled down on the performance of love – hoping if I were good enough, agreeable enough and loving enough, the heaviness would lift.

But it didn't.

And I stayed. Even after my body began whispering – louder and louder – that it didn't feel safe ... I stayed. Not because I was trapped. Not because he was a monster, but because I genuinely believed that staying was strength. I thought strength looked like loyalty. Like compromise. Like proving I could 'handle it'. I thought that if I just gave more, loved more, softened more ... things would get better.

But my body knew. My body flinched when he reached for me. My breath caught when he kissed me. I stopped initiating, stopped laughing and stopped feeling at home in my own skin. And still – I let him touch me. Not because I wanted it but because I believed I *should* want it. Because I didn't yet understand that consent is something you give moment by moment, breath by breath.

At the time, I didn't even know I *had* boundaries – let alone that I was allowed to honour them. Subconsciously I thought being a good woman meant giving myself over. Subconsciously I thought pleasing others was the highest form of love. I didn't realise I was abandoning myself in the process.

This wasn't empowerment. This was suffering dressed up as devotion.

The Mirror That Sparked My Reawakening

In the quiet ache of disconnection between who I used to be and who I'd become, something stirred.

An old lover from twenty years earlier reappeared with a simple message. It started innocently. A flicker of nostalgia. A remembering. What began as a soft reconnection soon grew into something that pierced deeper. He had once adored me. Desired me. Seen me. And in that season of my life – where I was still in my marriage, still saying yes when I wanted to say no and still living more from obligation than desire – his attention felt like oxygen. Not because of who *he* was, but because of what *he awakened* in me.

It wasn't about having an affair. It was about being reminded that I *was still alive* beneath the layers of numbness and sacrifice. I'd buried the woman who used to flirt, giggle and glow with sensual aliveness. His words, his longing, his presence – they cracked me open.

For a while, I clung to it. The playful texts. The emotional intimacy. The feeling of being chosen. But eventually, I realised: he wasn't the destination.

He was the mirror.

He showed me the version of myself I'd abandoned beneath marriage, motherhood and martyrdom. And when I saw her again – radiant, desired, sovereign – I knew I didn't need him to feel her.

I ended the connection with clarity and compassion because it had served its purpose. He wasn't my future. He was my reminder.

From that moment forward, I chose to be the one who kept that flame alive.

Reclaiming Pleasure as a Sacred Practice

Once I realised I didn't need someone else to awaken my sensuality, I turned inward – with intention, reverence and curiosity.

Pleasure stopped being something I performed or proved for someone else. It became mine. Sacred. Holy. Alive.

I began to treat self-touch not as a means to an end but as a ritual of self-devotion. I lit candles. I slowed my breath. I used oils that made my skin sing. And I stopped rushing.

For the first time, I let myself *feel* – not just physically, but emotionally and spiritually. I learned to hold space for myself in the same way I'd held space for everyone else.

Pleasure became a form of prayer. Not to an outside God, but to the divine within me. It reminded me that I was not broken. I was not too much. I was not dangerous. I was *powerful*.

Through breathwork, embodiment practices and sacred solo pleasure, I built new intimacy with myself. I began to trust my body again – not just to feel good, but to guide me. I learned what 'yes' felt like in my tissues – and what 'no' did too.

Pleasure became my teacher. It was no longer a reward or a secret. It was my birthright.

And in reclaiming it, I reclaimed *me*.

Letting the Old Burn

There's a sacred moment in every woman's reclamation where she realises she cannot carry the old identity into the new life. Mine came not with drama or destruction, but with quiet knowing.

I couldn't go back – not to the old dynamics, not to the old marriage and not to the version of myself who tolerated what her soul had outgrown. This wasn't about blame. It wasn't about hate. It was about truth.

I had outgrown the skin I was in. The roles. The silence. The people-pleasing. The performing. I was grieving the life I'd built – and honouring the woman I was becoming.

I left my marriage with as much grace as I could find, although it wasn't without ache. We tried to stay respectful. We chose a nesting model for the sake of our children. We committed to co-parenting with love, even when the love between us had changed shape.

I agreed to all of that, but more than anything, I committed to *me*. To no longer abandoning myself in the name of harmony. To no longer shrinking so others could feel comfortable. To no longer sacrificing my pleasure, truth and expression for someone else's approval.

This was the beginning of radical self-loyalty.

And like all sacred fires, it burned – but it also cleared the way.

The Path Back to Pleasure and Into Purpose

Coming back to pleasure wasn't a straight line. It was a spiral.

Some days I felt radiant – alive in every cell.

Other days I met the raw edges of grief, guilt or doubt.

But, as I kept practising sacred self-touch, embodiment and daily devotion, something else began to wake up: **my calling.** I realised my pleasure wasn't meant to stop with me. It was meant to ripple.

Seeing the Pattern

The more I honoured my body, the more clearly I saw how many women around me were quietly starving for the same thing. They had people-pleased their way into exhaustion. They mistook endurance for strength and called it love. Their libido had crashed under the weight of duty, shame, and self-loathing. They measured worth by productivity, not by aliveness.

These women weren't broken and they didn't all need to leave their relationships. What they needed was **permission** to feel, to want and to say yes *and* no with equal power.

Becoming the Permission Slip

I began to share.

First in whispered conversations with clients on the massage table: "What if pleasure could be a birthright, not a bonus?"

Then in workshops, circles, and retreats: We breathed together, moved together, reclaimed 'yes', redeemed 'no' and rewrote the idea that sensuality is dangerous.

I watched women soften, then rise – still married, still mothering, still working – but now anchored in their own power. Their relationships often evolved for the better: clearer boundaries, truer intimacy, renewed desire born from authenticity rather than obligation.

Purpose-made Flesh

My body became my teaching credential.

Every time I chose pleasure over performance, I offered living evidence of what I taught.

Boundaries can coexist with devotion.

Desire can deepen commitment.

Self-honour can heal disconnection faster than self-sacrifice ever could.

I'm not here to tell women to abandon their lives. I'm here to help them abandon the lie that self-betrayal is love. Pleasure is the compass that guides us back to ourselves – so we can choose, relate, speak and touch from wholeness instead of from wounds.

This is the work now. Walking as a permission piece. Teaching women to treat their pleasure like the power source it is. Reminding them that when they prioritise their own aliveness, everyone they love benefits.

A woman devoted to her pleasure is a woman devoted to truth – and truth is the most healing force on Earth.

To the Woman Reading This

If you're here, reading this with your own story woven quietly beneath the surface of mine, I want you to know something:

You do not need to hit rock bottom to rise. You do not need a traumatic past to justify feeling disconnected. You do not need permission to reclaim your sensuality.

We live in a world that has asked us to trade our radiance for responsibility, our softness for strength, our pleasure for productivity.

But you are allowed to want more. To crave intimacy – not just with others, but with yourself. To remember that you are made for joy, for sensation, for magic.

You are allowed to be both a masterpiece and a work in progress. To be wildly sensual and deeply spiritual. To speak your desires out loud and let them shape the way you move through the world.

You are not too much. You are not broken. You are not behind.

You are waking up.

And your pleasure is not selfish, it's sacred.

This is your invitation.

Not to become someone else, but to come home to who you've always been – the version of you who still believes in beauty, in softness, in power.

I don't walk ahead of you. I walk beside you.

Let's reclaim it. Together.

Xx Jo

Jo Goddard *is the founder of* ImHER Women's Wellbeing, *a sanctuary for women ready to reclaim their pleasure, power and self-trust. A certified sexological bodyworker, Kahuna massage therapist and women's wellbeing coach, Jo weaves body-based healing with soulful education to help women reconnect with their sensuality and inner wisdom. Her work is rooted in embodiment, emotional intimacy and radical self-love. As a speaker, writer and mother, Jo shares her lived experiences with raw honesty and compassion, creating space for others to rise beyond burnout, pain and people-pleasing into joy, truth and deep feminine liberation.*

Twelve Lessons

Laurel-Lea Jennings

Have you ever wished you could go back in time, for like twenty-four hours, and have an old-fashioned sleepover with your younger self?

For the sake of this story, imagine you're twelve years old.

You haven't quite hit puberty yet. Things are still relatively 'normal'. You have an ordinary routine – home, school, sleep – and boys are just starting to be on your radar. What would you say to your twelve-year-old self in that twenty-four hours? What lessons would you teach her? Would you tell her about all the heartaches she's about to go through? What about the medical treatments, hospital visits and trauma that's going to consume her twenties and thirties? Would you tell her to be strong and brave? Would you tell her things will never be the same again and that her life as a woman will never be what she expects it to be?

All that information, and more like it, would certainly be on my want-to-know list. Here's what I'd do with it.

As a child, you have this predisposed notion of what life will be like when you grow up. You watch other adults go through their day-to-day lives and you think: *Yep, that's going to be me one day.* You dream of having a respectable job, a great husband, a loving family and *lots* of kids. You play dress-ups with friends and pretend to walk down the aisle as brides. You pretend you're mummies with our thirteen dolls. You live your life so naive as to what the future holds and, when someone asks you what you want to be when you grow up, you proudly and succinctly say, "I want to be a mummy."

As you become a little older, you start planning what you want your life to be like.

You want to get that first job at fourteen. You want to earn money to save for a car and a house. By twenty-one, you want to be married to the love of your life. This gives you plenty of time to finish school and ensure you're healthy – ready for babies.

Being the eldest of four kids, you've always wanted a big family. In fact, you want to have three or four *beautiful* kids by the age of thirty. You want a house full of love, laughter, chaos and craziness.

What you don't know is that life will take you on some crazy paths – journeys that you'll never see coming. Life isn't going to be as clear and precise as you think it's going to be. At the age of twelve, you don't know that those life plans you're making in your head will be just distant dreams. You have no idea that you're going to have to *fight* for what you want; that people will be *mean* and bring you down every chance they get; that your body is going to *fail* you and that motherhood won't happen until you're in your forties – and even then, not in the traditional way you were hoping.

As a young woman, you get to know your body and how it operates. You learn about puberty and periods. You know how those *beautiful babies* you dream of are made. You think you understand what your bodies will go through when you have these *beautiful babies* and, eventually, good old menopause.

You know so much but what you're *not* told is what happens when things go *wrong*. You're not told that *you won't be able to do* the one thing you're taught that the woman's body is built to do.

I was thirteen when I got my first period. For about four months before D-day, I'd get the worst cramps. I thought I was *dying*. Mum would just shake her head and tell me to get to school. I'm sure she thought I was faking it. It was the end of school holidays and I'd just returned from a week at my best friend's grandparents' house. It was close to midnight. I felt *everything*: the sharp pains, the nausea, like I'd wet myself when, in actual fact, it was blood. I walked into my parents' room and shook my mum awake.

Me: *Mum, I'm bleeding.*
Mum: *What are you talking about?*
Me: *Mum, I think I have my period.*
Mum: *Pads are in my bathroom cupboard. You know what to do.*
Me: *Mum! It hurts!*
Mum: *Welcome to womanhood. Periods are painful so get used to it.*
Oh boy, was she right.

My periods were *so painful* I'd physically throw up. I'd shake and cry. I felt like the world was ending. None of my friends had their period yet, so I had no-one to talk to about this. As time went on, each of my girlfriends started to get theirs. Not even one of them had pain like mine. A little cramp here and there, sure, but nothing like I was experiencing.

Something was wrong.
This couldn't be right ... *right*?
What was wrong with me?
Me: *Mum, I think something is wrong!*

Mum: *What are you going on about now?*

Me: *Why am I in so much pain all the time? None of my friends are.*

Mum: *Everyone has different pain thresholds and maybe you just can't handle the pain as well as others. I'm in pain and you can't tell, right?*

Me: *Yeah, I guess. So, it's normal to get pain before my period comes and sometimes even after it finishes? It's normal to bleed for twelve days and have clots the size of fifty-cent pieces?*

Mum: *Well I do, so yes. Nothing wrong with me.*

If she had all this happening to her, then I guess it's just in my genes, right? Like mother like daughter? Little did we both know, this was *NOT* normal.

Fast-forward three years: I'm sixteen years old and sexually active. My periods are still so heavy and irregular. They last for ten to fourteen days at a time and are so painful I physically can't move from my bed for days. Standing up straight causes me to scream and now I can add painful intercourse to the list. Being new to the whole sex thing, I originally put it down to 'tight vagina', but no, there was something wrong and I should've listened to my intuition.

I should've spoken up and gone to the doctor.

Lesson One

This isn't normal. This isn't normal. This isn't normal.

If I could go back, I'd repeat that to my younger self until she listened.

My final year of high school came and went with me trying to attend as much as I could. I struggled, mentally and physically. Mum didn't care. Sorry, let me rephrase that: Mum didn't *want* to hear about my pain because she, too, was in pain – every day. It took my *fa-*

ther, a man who knows nothing about periods, to finally say, "Enough is enough." He couldn't handle seeing his daughter in pain anymore, so he booked a doctor's appointment for me the next day and off we went. My GP sent a referral for me to see a gynaecologist in the city. I had bloods taken to rule out infection and sexually transmitted diseases (STDs), even though I told her I'd had this pain since before my period started. She wanted to just be thorough.

Lesson Two

Be thankful for your father.

This man loved me *so* much that he sat behind a curtain while a gynaecologist was 'elbow deep' in his daughter. He sat there and listened to the doctor asking his seventeen-year-old daughter about sex. Not once did he judge me. He listened as the doctor suggested that I may have a new thing called endometriosis – and that I should look at having a baby to stop to the pain.

The look on my father's face was priceless, but he sat, and he listened, and he took notes.

I'd tell my younger self to have more faith in her father and trust him with her thoughts and feelings; he might just surprise you!

I had my first laparoscopic surgery for endometriosis at the ripe old age of seventeen. It was the year 2000 and not much research had been done on this reproductive disease. Once again, this doctor told me that getting pregnant would help my pain because I wouldn't be menstruating.

"You only get pain when you have a period so stopping your period for nine months will give you some relief." That's what he said.

The guy I was with at the time was not 'baby daddy' material, so that was off the table. As much as I wanted to be a mother, this situation and this man were NOT in my plan. Life went on. I had some relief for a little while. On a good day, my level 20 pain went down to a niggling 5–6. I was put on birth control to help manage the excess bleeding, but I just bled through it, so decided to stop taking it. I'd had enough of the pain and decided that if I fell pregnant, it wouldn't be such a dreadful thing, but it never happened. There were a few times I thought I might be, but nope. It was just my endo playing games.

Lesson Three

Make better life choices when it comes to boys. (I'm sure we all have this one.)

Listen to your head, not your heart. (That's a whole other story.)

I had my second surgery two years later, and then another surgery two years after that. It seemed to be a never-ending cycle. I could almost predict, to the day, when everything would come crashing down. My GP became concerned that it was all in my head, so she sent me to speak to someone. Two sessions in and they could tell: *it wasn't*.

I didn't choose this. I don't want to be in pain. I'm not seeking treatment. I don't like being cut open and feeling exposed. I don't enjoy being pulled into my manager's office at work to be reprimanded because of all the time I'm having off work. *No-one understood* because *no-one could physically see* what was wrong. It was inside me. I was broken and I didn't know how to fix it. Nothing was working. Surgery was a temporary fix.

Lesson Four

Don't let people get to you.

They'll be nasty. They'll say things that will cut you to your core – but be strong. You know what's happening. You know your truth and that's all that matters.

Fast-forward to twenty-two. I'd just broken up with my fiancé because, not knowing how long it would take, I wanted to try for a baby. He didn't want kids yet and felt like I was pressuring him. I was onto my fourth surgery and each time they went in, they found more and more endometriosis and adhesions from all the previous surgeries. I needed a change. I needed to get back *home* where I knew I was safe.

Lesson Five

<u>D</u>on't be in a hurry to leave home.

Running away from your family is not the answer. When you are young, all you want to do is grow up and move away. The constant bitching and issues with siblings – it's all going to be something you miss one day, when it's gone. Your family is the only place you'll ever feel safe and loved to the fullest.

I started a new job. After being with the one company for eight years, it was scary but also like a breath of fresh air. In my interview, I was open and honest with them about my health. I knew there was a chance they'd put me in the 'too-hard basket' – but they didn't. I got the call before I even left the carpark.

Starting over was *hard*. To go from being engaged, planning my future, seeing my lifelong dream of being married, with kids *so* close to coming a reality and then have it all turned upside down. I was now living in a share house. I had a new job. I was single – and *still* in pain. I made some new friends and started to find myself again. Once again, I was back in for more surgery. I started seeing one of the sales guys at work and things got intense – *very quickly*. I basically went over for a movie night and never left! I had to come off 'the pill' due to complications, so we tried to be careful. The Universe had other plans. A month into our relationship, I missed my period. I felt weird and didn't know what to do. I rang my best friend and she told me to do a pregnancy test. I freaked out that I was going to lose him. We'd only been together a month and I had no idea what he wanted in life. I didn't know if he wanted kids.

As I waited for the test results, I called him. I didn't even make small talk; I just ripped the Band-Aid off.

Me: *Hey it's me. I think I'm pregnant.*

Him: *Wow. Okay. Wow. OMG, that's amazing!*

Me: *What?*

Him: *I mean, I love you and if you are – then it's going to be amazing.*

Insert me sobbing

Me: *I love you too. There's a faint line. What should I do?*

Him: *Make a doctor's appointment. Do you want me to come with you?*

Me: *No, it's okay. I'll make one now. I'll let you know how I go.*

What the hell just happened?

Did he just get excited about babies?

I made a doctor's appointment but couldn't get in for a couple of days. In the meantime, my period started. He seemed disappointed but we now had to talk about where this was heading.

Lesson Six

Don't be afraid or hide what you want or who you are to please other people.

It's going to hurt you and it's going to hurt them. Be open and honest about your hopes and dreams, your goals and your fears.

Two months after our first pregnancy scare, we were engaged and, twelve months to the date, we got married. (FYI – we're still married, going on nineteen years.)

We made an appointment with my specialist to discuss falling pregnant and what it meant with all my broken bits. What would trying to fall pregnant look like for us? This is where the beginning of our seventeen-year journey to parenthood began. Blood test after blood test. Ultrasounds, tablets, injections, more surgery. You think it – **we tried it**. My arms were black and blue from blood tests on our wedding day. Thank God for make-up.

Two months after our wedding, I went in for a procedure to check my tubes for blockages. On my next cycle, I fell pregnant! It was real! Blood tests proved it, and I had the worst morning sickness – I felt awful. I had my bloods checked regularly and everything was going great. We traded in both our little cars and got a family car. We put car seats on lay-by and bought a pram. We told *everyone*. And when I say *everyone*, I mean including every single customer we served at work, whether they wanted to know or not. Our eight-week scan was getting closer, and we **couldn't wait**. I started having some pressure in my pelvis. Doctors reassured me it was normal and, due to my endo adhesions, pregnancy could feel different for me.

My sister had just found out she was also pregnant, and she didn't have anything like that.

Lesson Seven

Trust your instincts – even if you're wrong.

It's okay to be wrong. Speak up. Make people listen to you when you feel something isn't right.

Going into our eight-week scan, I felt empty. I hadn't had morning sickness for two days. I felt like I was getting my period. That heaviness in my uterus just wasn't going away.

Them: *I'm sorry but there's no heartbeat. You'll have some cramping over the next couple of days but if it gets too bad then head up to the hospital. They'll need to make sure the miscarriage is a complete one.*

Me: *How did this happen? Wait, what do you mean miscarriage?*

Them: *It happens more than you think. Most women will have at least one but then go on to have a heathy pregnancy afterwards. Just rest up.*

Yep, she said that.

Just. Rest. Up.

I was so angry. I couldn't stop crying. By the time we left the ultrasound, I'd started spotting. I was screaming at my husband, "They made a mistake. This isn't happening. There must be something we can do! Take me to the hospital."

Off we went. We went up to the maternity ward and a midwife sat us down to talk about what was happening. They took some bloods to check my human chorionic gonadotropin (HCG) levels. They'd dropped – almost to the point where they were back to zero. The pelvic pain I'd been experiencing for over a week was my baby dying. I passed the sac and life went on. I put all my energy into my new baby nephew. It was the start of the greatest love story known to humankind. Even today we have a bond like no other.

I look at him and wonder what our baby would've been like and the friendship they would've had.

Lesson Eight

It's okay to get angry.

Don't feel like you need to hide your emotions. Get angry. Get frustrated. Yell and scream if you must. Emotions show how passionate we are about something. Emotions mean we care.

I didn't yell or scream. I kept everything bottled up inside. I pretended life was peachy and just got back to my life. Work. Home. Rinse. Repeat.

We kept trying naturally for a while. We used the timing method. I tried different teas. I even tried acupuncture. The jig was up and we needed some professional help. My specialist said it would take some time to fall pregnant but this was getting ridiculous. We already knew we could fall pregnant but it wasn't happening. My endo had blocked one of my tubes, so we were already down a team player. We spoke to four different fertility specialists before coming across one who was willing to help us. My condition made it hard and no-one wanted to treat us.

They knew what we didn't know yet and none of them told us. Our new doctor monitored my cycle for three months before recommending intrauterine insemination (IUI). We tried three rounds and nothing worked so off we went – down the in vitro fertilisation (IVF) route. In the meantime, this doctor ran a test to check my egg reserve – or Anti-Müllerian Hormone for those playing at home. I was only twenty-seven or twenty-eight by this stage, but my ovaries were aging like a forty-five-year-old woman. My egg count was less than two.

I had no time left.

Lesson Nine

When you're seventeen and the doctor diagnoses you with endometriosis, ask your parents to pay for egg freezing.

Freeze as many of those suckers as you can because you're going to lose them before you can use them. If they say no, use the money you've saved up for a car. (Stuff the car, this is more important.)

I went down a *deep* dark rabbit hole after getting that news. IVF doesn't have the best odds on a normal day but this was going to be tough. What if they couldn't get any eggs out? What if I was barren? Is he going to leave me because I can't have kids? Why am I being punished? What have I done in my life that was so bad I deserved to have this ripped away from me?

My husband was promoted so baby stuff temporarily took a step back for us. Then, we made the leap to a new specialist who was known to take on the hard cases.

At egg collection, he retrieved two eggs. I was pumped with so much medication. If a normal twenty-eight-year-old woman went through this, she probably would've died from ovarian hyperstimulation – and *all I got was two*.

Once fertilisation takes place, they prepare you for the worst. They say there's a fifty per cent success rate. That left us with only one. But something was finally going our way because we had two healthy BB grade embryos. We decided to do a fresh transfer and freeze the second one.

It didn't work.

I started bleeding two days after transfer. Six months later, we transferred the frozen embryo. Everything seemed to be okay. No spotting. No pain. Just a weird fuzzy feeling in my uterus. The day before my fourteen-day blood test, I started bleeding. I ended up in hospital and they monitored me for a couple of days. I passed the sac and opted not to get another D&C.

I was done.

I didn't want to do this anymore.

We spoke about the possibility of adoption. We filled out our expression of interest paperwork and submitted our application with eight letters of recommendation from family and friends, telling them how deserving we were to be parents. My nephew even wrote a letter. Things progressed slowly. Our case worker changed as often as we changed our underwear. I sent an email asking what was happening because they only allow to you be on the first waiting list for two years before you have to start the entire process again.

Then, on one glorious day in June – I use the word 'glorious' because if I told you what I really want to call it, I may be banned for life – this happened:

Me: *Hello, Laurel-lea speaking.*

Her: *Hi, it's … from Queensland Department of Child Safety, Youth and Women. Is now a good time to speak?*

Me: *Absolutely. I just finished work and my husband is standing right next to me.*

Her: *Great that I have you both. So, after reviewing your application, we will not be progressing it any further.*

Me: *I'm sorry, what? Why? I don't understand.*

Her: *We feel that birth parents wouldn't pick you as your husband is too old and you're too big.*

Me: *I have a medical condition that messes with my hormones. I'm not always this big. I have endometriosis – and my husband is forty-three. That's not old. What are we supposed to do now? This was our last chance to become parents. I can't have children naturally.*

Her: *I am sorry for this, but you're just not viable applicants. If it doesn't happen – maybe you just aren't meant to be parents?*

Insert the deadest silence you've ever experienced

How did I go from FaceTiming my nephew for his eleventh birthday to sitting in my car – in my garage with the engine running – hoping that God would take me away from all this pain.

"... maybe you're just not meant to be parents."

This was on repeat in my head. Maybe she was right?

Lesson Ten

Get up and fight.

Fight like you've never fought before. You want this. You're going to have to go out and make it happen. You're worthy. You're meant to be a mother.

My husband gave up after that call, but I didn't.

I researched all the different ways to have a child in Australia. I had dreams about babies being dropped at our doorstep. I could hear crying one night and I checked the front door like a looney, thinking that a stork had dropped off our baby. I wanted to be a mum so bad *it hurt* – more than my endo pain.

Fast-forward to Christmas 2018 and we were at work late, working on Santa photos when my husband's phone rang. It was one of his gamer friends who we'd known for ten years. She heard what had happened with the adoption and had also known about everything else we had been through. The next six words to leave her mouth changed our path forever.

Her: I want to have your baby.

She wanted to be our **surrogate**. She wanted to give up her body for us so we could become parents. I'd only briefly read about surrogacy in Australia, so I went down that rabbit hole once again and researched the crap out of it. I joined Facebook communities and spoke to lots of different people about it. Our first issue was to find a clinic where we lived that would take us on. The first clinic on my list said YES, and we didn't look back.

Lesson Eleven

You're going to be barren by thirty-five.

Yes, I said that.

You need to be strong. It's not what you planned but this is going to happen to you. You're going to be empty and there's nothing you can do to fix that. Your sister will come to the rescue though. She'll donate eggs so you can at least have a genetically similar child. Even after how you treated her growing up, *she will be there for you*. You will have seven embryos frozen; there will be options for you.

Transfer one failed.

By this stage, I was a pro at miscarriage but our poor surrogate had never experienced the loss of a pregnancy. She'd had two healthy babies with no complications. Watching someone else go through something so personal is hard, especially knowing that you're the reason they're there in the first place. I was numb to the pain by now, so I had trouble being there for her. I had to break down walls to hold space for her.

Lucky for us, transfer two took and nine months later our beautiful daughter, Elizabeth, was born. *I have never experienced a love like this before.*

Lesson Twelve

Motherhood will happen for you but not like you planned.

It will be *better*.

You'll be older and wiser and, even though your knees will fail you when you play on the floor and you become tired more quickly than a mum in her twenties, you have the life experience. There's more than one way to become a mother, and you'll journey through all of them. Holding your daughter for the first time you won't be thinking about being twelve years old and wanting to be pregnant and have six kids. You won't be remembering all the failed attempts at love and life. You won't be wondering why your body failed and why you're in constant pain every day. You'll glance into Elizabeth's eyes and say to her, "Where have you been hiding all my life?"

To my younger self – be proud of the woman you'll become; the mother that you'll be to Elizabeth. Be proud of the fight you'll fight to get her here. Know you'll make it through all the years of pain, doctors telling you it's all in your head, the surgeries, the losses and the failed treatments. Be persistent. Be patient. Be kind to yourself.

You're an amazing human and I'm so proud of you.

Laurel-lea Jennings is a forty-three-year-old mum of one who lives in Kingaroy but calls Brisbane home. After facing infertility for over twenty-five years, Laurel-lea has turned her experiences into a source of support and inspiration for others on similar paths. Through her writing, she shares both her struggles and her triumphs, hoping it offers comfort and solidarity.

Beyond her writing, which she hopes to share more of one day, Laurel-lea has been an active member of the National Breast Cancer Foundation's Community Fundraising Team for sixteen years and is deeply committed to raising awareness about their role. She believes that finding something you're passionate about will bring you some form of happiness – a lesson she embraced during her own health challenges and finding a new path to her joy.

Life may not always go as planned, but Laurel-lea embraces every twist and turn with resilience and optimism, always encouraging others to stop, re-evaluate, adjust and move forward.

Identity Unravelled and Reclaimed

Some Days I'm Magnetic, Some Days I'm Just Moisturised

BELINDA TRISIC

I didn't have a rock-bottom moment. There was no dramatic collapse, no triumphant comeback montage. There was, however, just a slow, quiet unravelling – the kind you almost don't notice until everything feels off and until you're staring at your own reflection thinking, 'When did I disappear?'

Somewhere between perimenopause, old heartbreaks I'd never really voiced and a life full of holding space for others, I realised I couldn't see 'myself' anymore. Not the woman I'd worked so hard to become. Not the girl I used to be. Just this version in the middle – bruised, unravelling, quietly becoming.

For years, I'd survived things people didn't see. A marriage laced with control and gaslighting. Partners I loved who couldn't love themselves enough to heal. Children whose pain I couldn't fix. Generational trauma that seeped into every member of my family. I learned to hold it all gracefully and silently.

I kept showing up through it all ... until my own reflection started asking, 'What about you?'

This period of my life didn't come with one big all-encompassing answer neatly tied up in a bow. It came in a series of chapters. It also came with one persistent question I couldn't ignore: What would it look like to choose yourself fully?

This is the story of how I started saying yes to that. Not perfectly. Not all at once. But with small and deliberate intentions, a reclaimed voice and a growing belief that maybe – just maybe – midlife isn't a crisis but the cosmic kick in the pants we need to start choosing ourselves.

Part 1: The Slow Unravelling Begins

Why, as women, do we turn thirty-five and start to question all the 'should be, could be, would be' issues?

We're tired of the invisible labour and emotional scars. We're battle weary and body sore. We've done the therapy, healed our inner child, soothed our mad as hell 'inner teen' and met ourselves. We're honest, raw and revealed.

We start to recognise that we've been living out subconscious narratives – our narratives and those belonging to others. We realise we've been crafting versions of ourselves to impress, endure or survive. And slowly, we start unravelling all the expectations and box-checking, deeply and defiantly questioning all the choices, people and places that have led us to this point.

We are learning to let go of the 'good girl' and to start listening to the 'wise woman'.

Part 2: The Backstory I Didn't Want to Talk About

For me, that started with learning to heal the wounds and not pick at the scars of past relationships. I had a history laced with narcissistic relationships featuring addictions, control and depression. These were relationships I thought had depth, only to realise this 'depth' was actually a pit that I fell into trying to rescue them. They were also the relationships where the devil was in the details of the life I was living, and I was so ashamed to admit the mistreatment I was enduring that I continued until I couldn't anymore. These relationships not only cost me financially and emotionally but, worst of all, cost me my peace.

I would finally leave and start to claw my way back to myself. One tear in front of another until I was all cried out and left with nothing but the memories and the scars. Then, I'd take the little shards of my soul and, like a jigsaw, gently and lovingly put them back together.

Sometimes, I endured relationships in which I was receiving hurt from people who couldn't or wouldn't heal themselves. Some of the relationships were ones I'd been part of since childhood. These ones taught me how to read the energy in the room, feel every small shift in direction, keep low and quiet and not take up space that should have been mine.

But it was okay. I'd become used to being the strong one – the fixer, the quiet sufferer. It was a role I'd let myself become inherently familiar with. It was like an old threadbare sweater, held together only by the stitching of the seams.

It's no wonder that when midlife came knocking, I couldn't hear my own needs. I'd had my volume turned down for years.

Part 3: The Learning

My first thirty-seven years of life caused a tidal wave of learning.

Learning to let go of the apology that was never coming, the shame and guilt of not standing up for myself, and the hurt that no longer had a home inside my body.

Learning to hold space for myself, to remain soft and open, to find my voice and to create a life that all the versions of myself to date could be proud of.

Learning to find peace in the home I created piece by piece, in the beautiful souls who encouraged me lovingly and in the quiet moments where I could sit with a coffee in the morning sun and hear the rumbling snores of little dogs at my feet who felt that same peace.

Part 4: The New Me – Identity Crisis and All

Bathed in that peace, I started to make big, bold, life-altering choices. Ending a seven-year relationship, selling a successful hair, beauty and make-up salon that I'd been growing for over twelve years and suddenly finding I was ready for a new direction in a career I'd spent twenty years perfecting.

I casually joked it was my midlife crisis as I didn't know how to process the shame and embarrassment every time I had to tell someone I was now unsure of my future. As a woman who'd always been very decisive, mildly ambitious with a workaholic attitude and a just-won't-quit mentality, it was wildly disconcerting to find myself in a place with no business, no relationship and no direction.

So, I gave myself the gift of twelve months. Twelve months to realign, refocus and rebuild. No heavy decisions, no pressure and no creation from force. Just a whiteboard and a marker to write down every idea, every dream and every desire. Twelve months to be able to just sit with it all. Patiently. A year to learn how to slow down the hustle and lean into the uncertainty.

First came the guilt. The overwhelming drudgery of learning to be okay with being 'unproductive'. The task of unlearning the 'glorification of busy' that had been my life, and the constant mental maths of accounting for every minute to ensure maximum productivity and efficiency.

Next to arrive was the anger. The comparison of why my life had been spent learning to survive. Others seemed so easily to find a beautiful relationship in their early twenties, buy a house, have nice holidays and live what looked like picture-perfect lives, while I was just busy peeking through the windows. The old 'comparison is the thief of joy' was never truer.

Lastly, I met grief. When you stop long enough to feel all the emotions you'd stuffed into old boxes and hidden in the dusty corners of your soul, grief begins to knock at the door, begging to be felt.

I rolled up my sleeves and got to work unpacking a lifetime of old hurts, old stories and old beliefs. I held each one with care and consideration. I honoured every piece, thanking them like Marie Kondo for what they'd done to protect me and hold me. And then I let them know it was now time for joy.

I thought I'd nailed it. I thought I'd healed generational trauma, curated a loving home and invested in people who built me up. I said yes to every adventure – trips away with the girls, living our motto 'nothing surpasses the beauty and elegance of a bad idea' and getting tattoos to mark the occasion. I road-tripped enough to make a grey nomad jealous and motorcycled all over New South Wales with a bad-arse group of gals all. This was it; I'd unpacked my trauma, found my light and lived for joy. Smug little me thought I'd single-handedly cracked the code.

Then it began ...

Part 5: The Descent Into Chaos

At thirty-eight, I started to feel my body change. It wasn't like the movies that had all the menopause jokes but I was definitely the punchline. It was a quiet whisper at first, small insignificant changes that could be reasoned away as low iron, elevated thyroid levels, stress and so on. It moved in slowly. So gradually, it was almost undetectable. I wanted the aircon on while others were freezing. I turned down the hot tap on my shower, which had been an inferno burning off the remains of the day.

By thirty-nine, things were starting to become stranger. The immense weight gain. I'd always been a curvy babe but this was different; I was losing my waist with every kilo. The skin, which had always been kind to me, was becoming more and more unbalanced. Eczema and breakouts were my new winning combination. My hair was becoming curlier and drier; it was losing its lustre fast. Sleep became a moody ex – sometimes it showed up, mostly it ghosted me. A missed period (which had never happened in my life) caused a mass crisis and endless Googling of 'how many women don't know they are pregnant?' I even started listening to urban myths, and the true-story legends about women suddenly going into an unknown labour and having a child were living rent-free in my head. I armed myself with rapid response test after test, desperate to find out it wasn't due to a pregnancy.

Then it really started to kick in. All aboard the hot mess express. The hot flushes that left sweat trickling down like TLCs waterfalls. The under-boob sweat and heat rashes that no new bra could fight off. Nature's most cruel joke: a sudden reaction to antiperspirant that I'd been using for years and developing a rather strange body odour that no-one warned me about. There was also the crippling anxiety – weird things, like driving my car (which I'd always loved to do), suddenly made me terror-stricken. Riding my motorcycle, an activity that had always been a great source of joy, made me feel so anxious I had to give it up.

This sudden mistrust of a body that had done okay by me made me feel even more disconnected from myself.

At this point I couldn't remember anything. I had calendars and alarms for everything. I felt like I was losing my mind.

And the guilt! Sweet baby Jesus, the guilt! I couldn't remember to do things friends had asked of me or respond to texts. I was now doing some mobile hair and beauty work but forgetting to charge for some services. It was becoming a problem I didn't know how to solve.

Part 6: Send Help!

My first thought was that my anxiety had flared up, although I couldn't understand why. My life was the best it had ever been. Despite being unsure of a traditional future, I was living in the present moments. I was fully embracing the uncertainty and the joy that was on offer.

It made no sense and I was mad as hell. The woman in the mirror looked familiar but she definitely wasn't on the guest list. I'd done so much work to live in alignment with my anxiety so how could this be happening? The breathing, the mindfulness techniques, the filling up my own cup first – none of it was working anymore.

I approached my doctor and explained that I had genetic inheritance of starting menopause early. But, I was told I was too young and that, if anything, I might be in the very beginning stages. So I settled for anxiety medication. The hot flushes were due to anxiety attacks. The headaches from grinding my jaw, the insomnia from an anxious mind, the upset stomach and constant diarrhoea – all from tummy knots.

Spoiler alert! It wasn't enough.

Twenty unwarranted kilos and six months later, my doctor agreed to test. What they don't always explain is that the general tests don't show a lot until you're in a full hormonal upheaval, teetering on the edge of existence and questioning all your life choices. Apparently, there are now sixty-six diagnosed symptoms of perimenopause and, being the quiet achiever, my body was aiming to tick all the boxes.

At thirty-nine, it was official. My oestrogen had taken a one-way trip to see-ya-later-town and I was in early perimenopause. And it got worse; endless hot flushes, headaches, insomnia, diarrhoea, incontinence, more weight gain and the ultimate trifecta – rage, depression and anxiety.

The isolation and loneliness you feel in this phase is truly awful. Friends hadn't experienced this yet. Mothers and grandmothers didn't talk about it. Doctors aren't always educated about it. You feel like you're silently going mad. The tears are real and you're left only with Google and social media to grasp at straws of information to try and understand.

Feeling alone and confused, I decided to assemble a team of health professionals – body workers, energy healers, kinesiologists, chiropractors, naturopaths and massage therapists. I tried to tackle it from every natural angle possible. I was taking so many pills I rattled when I walked. But I persevered. Three years of natural therapies and another twenty kilos gained I was exhausted.

At almost forty-two, a new doctor and more testing showed my oestrogen had not only taken a one-way trip but she'd taken all her cousins, aunts and uncles with her. My hormones were in complete upheaval.

Part 7: Full-body Betrayal

The most ironic part was I'd spent over two decades helping women look and feel amazing. I was a beauty therapist, hairdresser, make-up artist and image consultant. I'd created multiple businesses, worked in editorial, taught my skills to peers, trained apprentices and lived, breathed and bled for the aesthetic world.

I was the friend that everyone came to for hair and beauty advice. The woman with a million 'just in case' outfits. I'd had pretty great hair and skin and was aging gracefully.

Suddenly I felt like a fraud. I was so lost. This wasn't the midlife crisis I'd heard about. There was no red sports car or hot young man. This was a full-blown identity crisis. Deep, disorientating and dark.

I didn't know what to do. I didn't want to reinvent myself – I just wanted to recognise myself.

I stopped investing in myself. I thought I was no longer worthy of looking and feeling great. My outward appearance was a direct reflection of how I was feeling. Every cell in my body was telling me I'd somehow failed myself. I kept reiterating to myself that if only I could 'get it together' I'd be okay.

It didn't stop there. My inner critic became so loud I had to name that wench. 'Betty' was like every high school mean girl you've ever met. She'd put Regina George to shame. She was able to pull at every thread of my self-esteem and shatter any confidence I'd accumulated in this lifetime. She'd shout at me, "You're too chubby to wear that. You don't deserve to feel good. You shouldn't bother with skin care. You look old now anyway. Why would anyone listen to your advice? You can't walk the talk. Look at you, letting them down again." It went on and on.

My inner dialogue had been hijacked by a chorus of limiting beliefs that were narrating my life. Each one had a front-row seat to the unravelling of my identity – and I was the one handing out the tickets.

Let me introduce you to a few of the greatest hits – the ones that had been shaping my image, my energy and my self-worth more than I care to admit.

I'm not good enough to look my best or deserve attention.

I'd stopped putting effort into how I looked – not because I didn't care but because some part of me thought I didn't deserve to. Beauty and style were reserved for women who hadn't 'let themselves go'. I looked in the mirror and only saw flaws, so I avoided style, colour, flair and anything that might ask me to have presence. The inner dialogue was brutal: "You don't get to shine until you're better, smaller, prettier."

Energetically? I was giving lukewarm tea when I used to be tequila with a lime wedge. People didn't connect with me because I wasn't fully there. I was shrinking to fit a belief I didn't even remember subscribing to.

It's better to blend in and not draw attention to myself.

So I toned it down. I wore nothing bold. I played nice. I was the fashion equivalent of a waiting room. Unthreatening. Unremarkable. I didn't want to be seen because I didn't feel like I had anything worth seeing. The fear of being visible made me blend in so well I disappeared.

My vibration? Dimmed like a mood light on a low battery. No wonder nothing magical was finding me – I wasn't showing up to be found. Ironically, that inauthenticity is what people really feel. It's that sense that something's off but you can't quite name it. It turns out that hiding isn't a vibe.

You don't even know who you are anymore.

I wore a mask. A curated version of me that felt easier for others to digest. A series of black stretchy pants and denial. But – you can't build real connections when you're wearing armour. You can't be magnetic when your energy is filtered through people-pleasing. It creates a misalignment between the external appearance and internal self, and I could feel the disconnect. I was a knockoff version of myself.

I'm too old to wear certain things or express my true style.

I suddenly found myself saying things like, "I'm probably too old for that", as if the style police were waiting to issue a fine for showing up in a leather jacket after the age of forty. This belief sucked the joy out of dressing. I was policing my own creativity before anyone else even saw it. Vibrancy had left the chat.

With that kind of inner narrative, it's no wonder I stopped recognising myself. It wasn't just the hormonal chaos or the physical changes – it was a perfect storm of shame, fear and old beliefs that no longer fit.

And Betty? She was just the loudest of them all.

My self-esteem followed my hormones and ended up completely non-existent. I didn't want to go anywhere or see anyone. Every social invitation filled me with dread and panic. Every forced outing left me crying into cowboy boots that no longer fitted. I'd lost such a huge part of my self-expression, and it was heartbreaking.

I decided I couldn't live in the shadows of my former self forever. Something had to give and I was done waiting to feel like myself again. If I couldn't find her, I would create her – piece by piece, ritual by ritual – until the reflection started to look familiar. Betty had done enough damage. It was time to change the channel to a station that sounded more like compassion and less like sabotage.

Part 8: Reclaiming My Reflection

I rolled up my sleeves and started. Again.

Journalling, morning sun coffee moments, softness, breath, compassion and grace became my new lens through which I learned to speak to myself. A daily practice of being kind to my reflection. Treating my body with care and gentle reminders. The glow-up wasn't external yet. That came after I stopped apologising for taking up space.

I learned to recognise Betty's voice as soon as she started and slowly turned her volume down.

I got to work clearing the clutter of past identities – it turns out curating yourself involves more crying and decluttering than Instagram suggests. Once I'd started to listen to my soul and unpacked all those limiting beliefs, I turned outward. I began to think differently. Maybe the outside wasn't superficial; maybe it was sacred.

Enamoured with that ideology, I created an action plan for myself. A step-by-step guide for getting back to basics. I embraced everything I could to learn about image again. I reread every manual I'd ever studied, listened to every podcast and watched every YouTube over my morning cereal.

I decided to start with colour. I chose three colours to build a wardrobe around knowing they were in my Colour Season and easy to find. I decluttered my wardrobe according to that principle. Letting go of every piece that was tied to a past me that didn't belong in my future. And somehow, through the midst of a room covered in past identities, I learned that the simplicity of less also brought in a sense of freedom from the overwhelm.

Next was style. Giving myself a style guide for the figure I had now, I relearned shapes and silhouettes that worked. I incorporated styles that I still loved but in sizes that suited my new curves without shame or guilt. Pinterest boards of the new me started to emerge. Pieces of the past influenced what was to become – pin-up, rockabilly, western, classic, feminine and wild all had a place in this melting pot of new.

I still got it wrong. I ordered clothes in sizes too small or styles that didn't quite work for my new shape. But I offered myself forgiveness for making mistakes and a constant emotional and physical sort-through of items until my wardrobe worked. I dealt myself compassion and grace before judgement.

I changed my hair colour. Always having had bold or unique colours, I opted for a soft blonde. Being a gentle blonde somehow said I was also being gentle with myself while I worked this out. Every treatment or blow-dry became a reminder to honour my crown.

I designed a skin care plan that was simple. No more beating myself up to follow an extensive plan that would only lead to disappointment if unfollowed. Every step became an intentional ritual. Cleansing to remove the old and embrace the new. Moisturiser – an act of nurture and support.

I embraced a new make-up routine that worked with my evolving skin, investing in products that suited me now and colours that reflected my light.

Through this reset, I recognised that image isn't just aesthetic but also your energetic blueprint. It's your way of having presence, taking up space and showing up for yourself. It's your vibration put out into the world. When we're operating in that highest frequency, we have the flow to attract people, opportunities and lifestyles that we desire. We change the conversation for ourselves and give permission for others to do the same. We embody our authentic selves. That presence can be felt.

What I'd thought was a midlife crisis was actually a midlife awakening in full swing. It cracked me open and stripped me bare to build again.

Then, finally, I realised I wasn't alone.

Part 9: The Passion Ignited

Friends, family and clients started the conversation, whispering the same thing: "I don't recognise myself anymore."

They were all asking: How do I feel like me again?

These women were struggling with what I'd been navigating for the last few years. Cocktails, cuppas and kitchen bench chats saw a communal sigh of relief that they weren't alone. These changes were real, raw and brutal. Every disappearing waistline, breakout and thinning patch of hair was a collective experience and a shared place of pain.

I realised that this universal spectrum all women endure needed a plan. It needed a simple breakdown to help with the external changes and the inner alignment that this identity crisis brings.

How do I feel like me again? That question became my mission.

I started to create again. Taking every bit of knowledge gained over a twenty-year career and pouring it into a renewed purpose, *The Aligned Image Movement* was born. It was a beautiful by-product of my own healing.

This movement is for the women crawling out of their own hot messes. For the ones whispering, "Is it just me?"

No, babycakes, it's not. You're not alone.

Part 10: The Becoming

The honest truth is I'm still evolving. What my 'healing' looks like right now changes from day to day. Some days I'm on fire; other days I'm fumbling around with wobbly confidence like a baby deer on roller skates. There are moments of perfect clarity and days spent in pyjamas with the beauty of a slow morning to soothe my soul.

I've learned that compassion over perfection is the mantra I need to live within. Some days I'm magnetic; some days I'm just moisturised. But every day, I show up – even if it's just for myself.

And Betty? She still creeps in but recognising her and quieting her is easier now. I'm quicker to catch her snark and to choose curiosity over criticism. I remind her this home is no longer her stomping ground.

Now, I'm calling in visibility, softness, joy and community. I've stopped waiting for permission and started giving it to myself – to be seen, to take up space, to live loudly when I want and softly when I need.

I've discovered that 'becoming' is not a destination. It's a practice. It's a ritual. It's present in how I dress in a way that honours who I am now, in how I pour love into my business and creativity, in the friendships I nurture and the boundaries I set. It's found in the wild belly laughs and in the quiet moments I make space to simply breathe.

If you're still in the middle, keep going. You're not broken. You're not behind. You're becoming.

I promise you that your favourite self is still to come.

Belinda Trisic *is the founder of* The Aligned Image Movement *and creator of* The Aligned Woman Method, *where she blends image strategy with energetic alignment to help women 40+ rediscover their power, presence and purpose. With a background in beauty therapy, hairdressing, make-up artistry and image consulting, Belinda brings a unique lens to personal transformation – one that celebrates both style and soul. After navigating her own reinvention through early perimenopause, relationships and identity shifts, she's passionate about helping other women rewrite the rules of midlife. Through her signature programs, speaking events and online platform, Belinda empowers women to show up unapologetically, radiate confidence and reclaim the mirror as a tool of self-celebration rather than self-criticism. Belinda believes that when a woman aligns her image with her energy, she becomes magnetic – not just in appearance, but in life.*

When 'Normal' Isn't Right: Reclaiming the Wisdom of Your Body in Midlife

SALLY PATTISON

"*You're fine.*"

It was meant to be reassuring. But those two words made me want to scream.

I'd walked into the doctor's clinic fatigued, totally exhausted. I was waking in the early hours with my heart racing. My moods were up and down. I felt puffy, heavy, mentally foggy and disconnected from myself. I walked in with so many unexplained symptoms. I was full of questions and fears about what could be wrong.

But apparently everything looked 'normal'.

Bloods: normal. Thyroid: normal. Iron: normal. Hormones: 'just a bit perimenopausal'.

"So this time of transition will be for the next ten or so years. You'll come out the other end, eventually."

Except I didn't feel normal. I didn't feel *fine*. I felt like I was quietly falling apart inside my own body. I felt so dismissed.

I was in my forties – showing up for work, family, clients and commitments. Under the surface, though, something was off. I was crumbling. Sure, I was 'doing all the things'. I was eating well, walking every day and taking supplements. But something just didn't feel right. However, when tests are clear it's easy to second-guess your intuition.

Having twenty years in medical diagnostic imaging, I had the training. With over twenty years as a naturopath, nutritionist and herbalist – even with all my knowledge – I almost handed my power over to that one sentence.

"You're fine. Blood tests don't lie."

That was the moment I realised how easily women are dismissed in midlife. And how important it is that we start listening to ourselves.

For me, the symptoms grew, becoming more extensive. It was more than fatigue, there was the horrendous joint pain that stopped me from driving or even walking because of the sheer pain in my feet. I could feel every stone, every twig, underfoot. The crushing fatigue left me moving from bed to couch. My beloved garden went to wrack and ruin. My dog was going stir crazy with no walks.

That quiet whisper inside wouldn't leave me alone. Something was wrong. I just didn't know how to prove it or how to get to the bottom of what it was.

I went back to the doctor and then to the specialist. More tests 'to satisfy me'. And then ... some answers started coming in.

It was NOT all in my head! I had three viruses concurrently, which had triggered reactive arthritis. Then, mix that with the hormonal roller coaster of perimenopause and burnout.

Looking back, I see how burnout left my body vulnerable to illness and how the hormonal shifts of perimenopause amplified everything I was already carrying. The viruses were real and the arthritis was real, but so was the burnout that had worn me down after years of over-giving and ignoring my needs.

The suggestions – anti-inflammatories, seven cortisone injections (as well as oral ones) ... oh ... and some low-dose chemo.

No, thank you.

"You have fibromyalgia and reactive arthritis so that is the treatment for those conditions. The rest, well, you'll have to learn to live with them for now."

Like many women, I grew up learning to be agreeable and to trust authority figures – teachers, doctors, 'experts' – more than I trusted myself. I was taught to be 'good', not make a fuss and to certainly not challenge what a woman in a white coat told me.

I tried to believe the results.

I kept swinging between hope and despair.

The fatigue and the pain were overwhelming.

It wasn't just me. Over time, I saw this story reflected back in the women I supported: the collision of unacknowledged burnout with the hormonal transitions of midlife.

Midlife Is Not a Decline - It's a Reckoning

Behind all that was the 'midlife' dismissal.

As I entered midlife, I noticed a shift – not just in my body, but in my sense of identity. The things that used to work stopped working.

The rhythms I'd relied on began to change. Sleep patterns, hunger, mood, energy, libido – it all became unpredictable. And yet, when I spoke up about it, the response was so often:

"That's just menopause." "It's normal at your age." "Welcome to midlife."

But those answers, along with the other answer – it's just hormones – didn't bring me peace. It brought frustration. Why were we told to just accept this unravelling? Why were we not taught how to support our bodies *through* this powerful phase, rather than ignoring the signs? Midlife isn't a breakdown – it's a becoming. And that includes learning to advocate for ourselves, especially when the systems around us don't.

My symptoms were not random; in fact, they're words I've heard from so many women. Perhaps not the viruses but definitely the exhaustion, joint pain, insomnia, brain fog, lack of libido, bloating and weight gain, inflammation, mood swings, irritability, anxiety, lack of confidence ... the list is rather long.

Over and over again, I hear of women being gaslit by their GPs and it's not on. It's not okay.

Our bodies speak to us in whispers long before they scream. Fatigue is not laziness. Bloating is not weakness. Mood swings are not overreactions. They are all messengers – and they're asking us to listen.

When You Know, But They Don't Believe You

The most dangerous thing that can happen in midlife isn't weight gain or hot flushes or mood swings – it's losing trust in your own voice.

I remember thinking:

Maybe this is just how it is now.

Maybe I am overreacting.

Maybe I just need to push through.

But my body knew better. She was speaking to me through the insomnia, the bloating, the brain fog and the aching joints. She wasn't malfunctioning; she was asking me to pay attention.

This is where so many women lose themselves. We're told it's 'just hormones', so we downplay what we feel. We try to cope, push, suppress and override until our bodies force us to listen. And in the process, we disconnect from our inner authority. But your intuition is a diagnostic tool, too, and mine was screaming: *This isn't normal – it's common, not normal and not okay.*

What I've come to believe and what I now teach every woman I work with is this: You don't need someone else to confirm what you already know deep down. You don't need another supplement to fix something your intuition is already flagging. You don't need permission to take your own symptoms seriously.

What you do need is: the courage to keep asking; the support to be believed; and the tools to decode what your body is saying.

Above all else, you also need the reminder that you are the expert of your own body.

The Turning Point: Reclaiming My Power

Patients coming into my clinic echoed my own thoughts and experiences – the fatigue, the weight gain, the anxiety, irritability, insomnia … Listening to them was like having a mirror held up to myself. They too had been told they were 'fine' and that their symptoms were 'common' and would pass.

For me, it was less of a 'big bang' and more of a 'quiet whisper' that I finally answered. How was I able to support these women, but not listen to myself? I'd stopped caring for myself.

With this realisation, I started supporting myself the way I'd supported hundreds of women over the years with nourishment, nervous system care and deep listening. I remembered what I knew. I returned to the truth I'd taught others: symptoms are messages, not malfunctions.

Bit by bit, I reclaimed my rhythm. Not by doing more, but by finally tuning in.

The Myth of 'Normal' And Why It's Failing Women

There is a dangerous lie in midlife medicine – if your labs are normal, you must be well.

After two decades working in health, I knew lab results mattered but I also know that what a woman *feels* often tells a deeper story. Women are not lab results. You can be within range and still feel completely off. You can look 'fine' and be barely holding it together. You can have a healthy diet, exercise and good intentions – and still feel like your spark has gone missing.

This is not a failure. It's not aging. It's a signal.

We need to shift from diagnosing disease to recognising *imbalance*. From silencing symptoms to understanding them. From waiting until women break down to supporting them as they transition.

Midlife Is The Awakening If We Let It Be

Working with women in midlife, I've seen a pattern again and again: they're told to lower their expectations; they're told their exhaustion is normal; and they're told their loss of libido, weight gain, anxiety and brain fog are 'just part of the package.'

But what if they're not?

What if midlife isn't the beginning of the end, but the beginning of a new way of being?

What if this phase, with all its chaos, changes and discomfort, is the *invitation* we didn't know we needed? The one that says: Stop ignoring yourself. Start trusting your body. You don't need to prove anything anymore.

This isn't a breakdown. It's a return to rhythm, truth and self.

What I Want Every Woman in Midlife to Know

Looking back, I don't regret the journey but I wish I'd been given permission earlier. Permission to slow down. Permission to rest without guilt. Permission to say, "I don't feel like myself" – and have someone believe me. Permission to realise that 'normal' on a lab report doesn't always equal *optimal* health.

Symptoms speak louder than numbers on a piece of paper.

If I could go back to that woman sitting in the clinic all those years ago, I'd take her hand and say, "You're NOT being dramatic. You're NOT imagining things. You're NOT failing. Your body is wise and she's asking you to listen."

If you're in your forties or fifties and wondering if this is really 'just it', here's what I want to tell you: You're not crazy. You're not broken. You're not failing. What you're feeling is valid. Your symptoms are real. Your body is wise. And even if no-one else listens, you can.

Start asking better questions. Stop settling for dismissals. And never again give your power away just because someone says, "It's fine."

Your body is trying to protect you, NOT punish you.

This Is the Revolution: Self-Trust

This chapter isn't about me – it's about all of us.

The woman who's exhausted but still getting up at 5 am.

The woman who keeps being told her bloods are normal but can't get through the day without coffee and willpower (which we know fades).

The woman who's been trying to 'cope' her way through the chaos.

We've been coping long enough. It's time to rise – and that begins not with another prescription but with a pause. A breath. A decision to trust your inner knowing. You already have what you need. You've just been taught to ignore it.

Midlife Is Not the End – It's the Alchemy

This is not a crisis – it's a calling. To return to your rhythm. To honour your voice. To rewrite what midlife means, on your own terms. The world may tell you that everything looks 'normal', but if your body says otherwise, *believe her.* She's not asking you to fix her. She's asking you to *finally* listen.

What is your body whispering to you right now and are you willing to listen?

Sally xo (The Midlife Alchemist)

Sally Pattison *is your go-to hormone specialist and Midlife Alchemist. She's spent over twenty years as a naturopath, nutritionist and herbalist, helping women navigate midlife with confidence and calm, guiding them to reconnect with their body's wisdom and reclaim their inner power. Sally is passionate about empowering women to transform their health and lives naturally, especially through the midlife years and beyond. As a mum and grandmother, she knows the juggle and the joys of caring for others, but she's also learned how important it is to care for herself along the way.*

Cooking nourishing meals is Sally's love language, and growing medicinal herbs and creating a cosy, healthy family home bring her joy. When Sally's not tending to patients in her clinic or supporting women online, you'll find her reading, researching and exploring the latest science to help women thrive in midlife.

Sally's mission is to help women take back control of their health and wellbeing so they can feel vibrant, confident and at home in their bodies – because midlife is not the end; it's your alchemy.

Wherever You Go, There You Are - And That's the Point

Angela Heise

I learned to read at a very early age. By seven, I was devouring Greek and Egyptian mythology. Yes, I was a bit weird.

Fascinated with places different from where I was living, I decided that by the time I died, I wanted to have seen the whole world.

At ten, I went on my first school exchange with Coventry Blue Coat Church of England School. I had to be dragged back to Germany by the hair when it turned out that I resonated with the Anglo-Saxon acceptance of eccentricity and sense of humour far more than with the German focus on judging non-conformity and laughing about it from a place of Schadenfreude.

This was the beginning of a realisation that would build over the next years: I didn't fit into the environment I was growing up in. I was somehow different.

Over the next few years, my family life – which had always been dysfunctional, I just didn't know it—exploded into a new realm of chaos. There were suicide attempts, depression, and violent outbursts. Doctors handed out Valium like lollies, and nobody really knew what they were doing. I withdrew into my own realm, into books.

The city library saw me take home seven or eight novels, biographies, and non-fiction publications every week. I discovered the self-development and esoteric section and systematically worked my way through it. At the same time, I interviewed my grandparents about their history and what my parents were like growing up. I wanted to understand why people on both sides of the family demonstrated every day that they were invested in unhappiness instead of exploring what would create happiness.

The California Awakening

When I was sixteen, I had the opportunity to visit California. My father drove me two and a half hours to Amsterdam Schiphol Airport, where we discovered that my direct flight to Los Angeles had been overbooked and I had lost my seat. Naturally, my father's first response was to bundle me back up and take me home.

What followed was probably my first successful teenage act of putting my foot down. When the woman behind the counter offered to send me to New York, I jumped at the opportunity. I didn't care that I would have to navigate two terminals alone; I was ready for an adventure.

I successfully navigated a stern immigration interview, producing the invitation letter and return ticket to prove I wasn't planning to immigrate illegally. I dragged my suitcase between terminals and patiently waited while they repaired the plane to L.A., which finally took off with a five-hour delay. There were no phones, no-one knew where I was, and I had no idea if I would be picked up in L.A. I was completely free for the first time in my life. It was exhilarating.

I spent six weeks with an All-American family speaking only English, eating Mexican food, wheel-size pizza, and gigantic burgers balanced by Diet Coke. I learned that it was normal to drive an hour to a restaurant to eat food I could have easily and more quickly cooked myself. That we drove everywhere.

I came back to Germany understanding that rules were only rules because a group of people had decided they were norms. Like shaving your legs, a practice non-existent in Germany, but that prompted a massive intervention in L.A. before I was allowed to go to the beach a second time.

That summer, I learned that culture is just a set of shared illusions and that I didn't have to accept all of them. That I could choose.

My subsequent acts of rebellion, questioning why I had to do things the way everyone did, didn't go down well in a family deeply invested in fitting in and playing by German rules. One of their standard sayings was: "What will the neighbours think?"

University and the Quest for Understanding

I moved out to attend university at eighteen, not studying psychology, as I had wanted. My parents strongly objected. As my father put it, it would mean acknowledging something was wrong with our family. Since we were making sure to uphold every norm to look normal, I was denied that path, not realising life would take me back into this field later.

In another act of rebellion, I studied history and Chinese, hoping that learning about the past and a vastly different culture would help me understand the cultural norms that seemed to determine our lives.

The Roaming Years

The next fifteen years saw me studying in Beijing and California, working as a historian in New York, as an English teacher in Taipei, dealing in export in Austria and Germany, running a company in Hong Kong working all over Southeast Asia, producing TV in Germany, and eventually arriving in Australia, where I ended up managing an international alternative health seminar network. I did what I had promised myself as a child: I explored the world.

When Friendship Became Love

When I accepted the role in Australia, it didn't come from exploration like the other jobs. Instead of sitting on a plane thinking, "Oops, I forgot how much they're paying me—oh well, if I don't like it, I'll just leave," moving to Sydney was a deliberate decision to find a place where I could belong, working in a role where I could make a difference.

It was in one of the seminars I organised that I met a charismatic blond man, just as interested in self-development as I was. We had a great conversation over dinner, and he went back to New Zealand the next day while I settled into my new life in Australia. It was a lovely encounter, and that seemed to be the end of it.

Until he showed up to the next seminar carrying big boxes of belongings fresh from the airport. His company had transferred him to Sydney.

I had already organised a lift when L. mentioned he had moved to my suburb. We discovered our streets were adjoining, so he hitched a ride with us. When L. told my friend to stop the car, it turned out our houses were at the respective corners of the two streets, right next to each other! We could wave from our windows!

Over the next few weeks, L. and I spent a lot of time together. We were both settling into new roles and not knowing many people. We explored the neighbourhood and supported each other through the formalities of a new life in a new country. When we discovered our shared passion for backgammon, we played for hours and days. When we weren't rolling dice, we were listening to music or sharing things that mattered to us.

Anyone who suggested we would make a nice couple was told we simply weren't each other's type. I liked my men taller and dark; L. liked his women much less down-to-earth and practical.

The usual butterflies of sexual chemistry were noticeably absent, and so were all the other elements that usually came with the territory: I could meet L. makeup-free with hair standing in all directions; admit when I was sad, angry, or "off" instead of pretending to be cheerful; and I didn't have to second-guess his reactions to my communication.

Being with L. felt warm and connected, and our relationship grew closer. A few weeks later, we spent Saturday night in the usual way—time flying as we listened to music, played, and talked. I can't remember why we decided L. shouldn't go home, but I remember we were clear we weren't going to jeopardise our friendship for a fling when we weren't attracted to each other. We ended up sleeping on my brand-new sofa bed, fully clothed, holding hands.

The next day, we went to yoga, had breakfast, read the newspaper, and spent time on the beach. We were thrilled to finally find the rhythm of a typical Sydney Sunday. When we returned that night, L. came in only to pick up something he had left behind. An hour and a half later, we were still standing in the hallway talking when he suddenly leaned forward and kissed me.

I had always joked about the Frog Prince phenomenon—women falling in love with the myth of the frog who, once kissed, miraculously transforms into the prince. I was completely unprepared for the overwhelming sensations when L.'s kiss went far beyond a friendly peck. When I tried to find words for my experience, I struggled. This is the only way I can describe it: I heard bells ring and angels sing, and felt as if my blood had been replaced with sparkling champagne.

L. never went back to his place that night. The next morning, we developed a routine that shaped the following months: after breakfast, he would go back to his place to iron a shirt, put on his suit, go to work, come back to change into casual clothes, walk through the undercover car park into my apartment building, stop to take advantage of the acoustics and—as a budding opera singer—belt out an aria so I knew he was coming, then spend the night with me.

Marriage and the Desire to Do Things Differently

Living with L. was increasingly joyful, and we grew closer every day in the tiny apartment. Work, however, was a different story.

My boss, who had provided my work visa, seemed to feel she owned me. Having used up my meagre sick leave during an illness, I was no longer entitled to any days off. As part of the "calling," as she labelled it, I consistently worked at least three hours overtime daily, putting in weekend hours to catch up on paperwork and managing logistics for late-night seminars.

There was no time off in lieu. The better I performed, the greater the demands. The implication that nothing was ever good enough unless my boss did it herself was taking its toll on my self-esteem. L. and I decided to move up the wedding.

I had been working non-stop for months when I asked for a day off. It wasn't granted. Only my assistant knew it was my wedding day when I claimed a migraine shortly after arriving at the office. I picked up my bouquet from the flower shop around the corner, praying nobody would see me.

The wedding took place on the beach. We solemnly read vows we had written one Sunday afternoon on the office computer between filing papers, promising to support each other to be the best we could be as long as this love and commitment would last. I had refused to put "until death do us part" into our promises.

While our friends cried in the background, a group of punks watched and loudly applauded when we kissed. The photographer shot hundreds of photos to send to family and friends overseas. They show two very happy people, determined to create a relationship that would transcend any model we had learned from our parents.

L. and I were determined to have a different marriage. We knew our parents' model didn't work. We both had identified that the theme "commitment to an unhappy marriage" ran strong in both our families, and we agreed that repeating it was out of the question. The costs were simply too high. So we looked at what we wanted instead, not realising we would fall into the familiar traps and create the same thing. We had the goal; we just didn't know how to get there. The new territory we wanted to enter didn't come with a map.

When we told my boss we had gotten married, things got worse. Her demands skyrocketed, and between working, eating, and sleeping, the next month passed so quickly I almost forgot I was married.

Two days after I insisted on taking time off for a bad flu despite my boss's objections, I was diagnosed with chronic fatigue and went from working overtime to sleeping fourteen hours a day. For weeks, I had been saying I was "sick and tired of this job," and that was exactly what I got.

The world reflected how I felt by literally collapsing around me. Any conversation longer than five minutes exhausted me so much that I needed a nap. This was still supposed to be my honeymoon! Being carried from bed to toilet because my legs wouldn't carry me was not how I had imagined the beginning of my marriage.

The Slow Fade of Dreams

Dealing with sick people daily, I had learned early that I wasn't equipped to manage the problems people asked me to handle. I frequently left work feeling overwhelmed and helpless. To learn more—also preparing to raise our future children without passing on toxic patterns I had vowed to eliminate in my teens—I had started studying counselling and enrolled in a neuro-linguistic programming practitioner course when I got sick.

Over the following months, I went on a strict elimination diet, took daily handfuls of vitamins, meditated, and used my NLP training to work on my beliefs. I completely recovered.

When my doctor declared he must have misdiagnosed me, I didn't care about the label. I was healthy again, enthusiastically throwing myself into my marriage.

It was my choice to dissolve my savings fund—supposed to be our apartment deposit—to pay for L.'s tuition when he was admitted to the Opera Course at Sydney University's Conservatorium of Music, one of eight chosen from hundreds of applicants. We made a deal: he would get two years to study while I supported him, then I would get two years for film school while he supported me.

Within six months of being married, I had recovered from a major illness, quit my job, and was supporting a husband who spent most of his time fulfilling his potential while I renovated an apartment, keeping busy while waiting for my permanent residency and new work permit to be granted.

Despite all our awareness and self-development work, over the next years, I turned into someone I didn't like, displaying the same behaviour I abhorred in my parents. I care-took L. to such a degree that when I realised what I was doing, I almost threw up in disgust and horror.

Looking back, I can see how I gave up who I was, how I reduced myself to being in a marriage where we had committed to being the best we could be and support each other in fulfilling our potential. I just didn't work on fulfilling mine; instead, I reworked it so it would help L. fulfil his.

It wasn't dramatic; it was death by a thousand small accommodations.

What started as support to help L. overcome stage fright turned into a business when people saw how much he had changed. I honed my skills with willing clients—his singer colleagues, actors, instrumentalists, and anyone willing to let me practice. I planned my life around L.'s burgeoning career that, according to his singing teacher, could easily see him perform at The Met.

Since I observed numerous marriages between opera singers and their partners suffer through long absences and the intense opera world climate—where alliances and enemies are easily made and affairs blossom backstage—my life goal changed to becoming a stage fright expert, ready to travel with L. wherever he performed, with a ready-made clientele at every destination.

It took me several years to become aware of the fact that my dream had quietly died. That I had started to erase myself. Yes, I was still doing self-development courses and completing certifications in more self-development modalities to expand how I could support people, but they were all supposed to help us while L. sang at opera houses around the world.

Maybe it started when my father put my hand into my husband's and said, "She is your responsibility now," and gave us money to buy L. a piano. When I asked where that left me, his response was: "Sometimes you just have to let go of your dreams."

Ironically, I wasn't aware that I had abandoned my goal of working in film until years later. By then, our agreement that I would have my time for film school had long been lost. It simply wasn't an option anymore. We were building a life that couldn't accommodate two years of study.

The Decision Point

I was thirty-nine when I realised I didn't want children with L.

I had just returned from a two-month business trip in Europe to find that - from what I could tell - little had moved forward in my absence.

I was exhausted from what felt like holding up the sky – marketing, delivery, admin, budgeting – while L. appeared to reluctantly pursue the opera career he had declared his soul's vocation. I found myself nagging constantly and slipping into the controlling mother role I had observed in so many women around me.

I didn't want to take the risk of adding a child to an increasingly challenging dynamic. I also didn't know if I didn't want children altogether and would have to let go of my goal to heal the next generation

When I told L. about my decision not to have children, he said he didn't want children either, that he simply wanted to be married to me. I told him that, in my opinion, he needed children, given that his family values were built around them.

After all, we had sat with his family one Christmas looking at the family tree, and the patriarch had pointed at us, bemoaning that I was the only woman who had kept her last name and that we didn't have children yet.

I wasn't punishing L. for a family system that was built on tradition; I was stepping out of it so I wouldn't betray myself and could honour his.

We celebrated my fortieth birthday while living in separate apartments to give L. the opportunity to live by himself, which we both felt was important to reestablish the partnership foundation of our marriage. He didn't want another mother, and I didn't want to be one.

A few months later, we celebrated our eighth wedding anniversary. As we toasted with champagne, we looked at each other and almost simultaneously said: "This is our last anniversary, isn't it?"

We had a very amicable divorce without lawyers.

Shortly after, L. met a lovely woman who already had three boys. They quickly married, added more children, and for many years, I was part of the family, taking photos on special occasions and serving as another point of reference when the children needed one.

It turned out I was a great Auntie Angela, using my skills to make a difference to the next generation for my ex-husband's family and all my clients, who often said that they were glad that I didn't have children because it meant I could help them raise their children.

For me, not having children didn't mean walking away from love, care, or legacy.

Reinvention and Return

We are taught that by the age of forty, we should have 'arrived': career, marriage, identity, stability. But for me, life has kept unfolding, unravelling, and reshaping. The freedom that came post-divorce, while initially destabilising and scary, was incredibly liberating. I felt like myself for the first time in a long time, dropped the extra weight, and felt attractive in a non-Mum way again.

L. and I tried to keep the company going during our separation, but it became obvious within a few months that our established pattern hadn't changed: I handled most of the background work while L. delivered the services. The difference now was that we no longer shared the fees. As the visible face of the business, L. continued to receive contracts while I struggled to pay rent. Everyone assumed I was thriving because I hid my struggles. My grief over our lost relationship and its potential wasn't as visible as L.s - I didn't just look functional, I was functional. As my friend called it, I suffered from the curse of the competent.

When I realised that the business model was not sustainable, I started my own company and developed my own training and coaching framework for both professional and personal growth. Solely responsible for myself. It took me a few years to work my way out of the STD I had come out of the marriage with: sexually transmitted debt.

L. and I had very different ideas of what financial stability meant, another reason why I didn't want children with him. It was simply not enough for me to know that we had enough money in the bank to pay the rent. Living from one minimum credit card repayment to the next was not my idea of a sustainable lifestyle.

To completely draw the line between L.'s and my finances, I asked my father, who was already disgusted that I hadn't stuck it out, for a loan, so I could pay my part of the debt off. He initially turned me down, finally consenting after I put together a business proposal and offered to pay him back with interest. Which I did.

I had just found my feet when I got sick and went into debt again. Thankfully, I was lucky to have a good friend who told me that she was tired of watching me pay off debt and that I needed to get into a saving mindset. So she cleared the money I owed, and I started paying her back into a savings account, where I could see the balance go up instead of down.

While I was changing my mind about debt, I did some deep work on worthiness and being good enough, stepped up, and consequently secured some big jobs. Soon, the savings account showed I had made good on my promise.

Global Nomading

For a long time, I had challenged myself to learn something new or stretch myself every year. When my landlord terminated my lease, I had just finalised my overnight allowance for tax purposes and discovered that I had spent 278 days away from home. The decision to see what it would be like to live out of a suitcase for was instantaneous. I put everything into storage and labelled three suitcases 'cold', 'moderate' and 'hot' that I repacked depending on where I was going.

The decade that followed became my true nomadic phase, as I worked for a couple of big companies that sent me all over Australia to conduct leadership and emotional intelligence workshops and coaching programs. I lived out of my suitcases for over four years, sleeping in close to 300 beds, flying on hundreds of planes. I also travelled the world and visited places I had always wanted to see.

On a two-week trip to see Cusco, the Nazca Lines and Machu Picchu, I fell in love with Peru and ended up living on and off in Lima for over nine months, exploring the country and learning Spanish. I knew that even though I had a strong sense of belonging, Peru wasn't a permanent home. However, it was a place where I could reconnect with my adventurous side as I travelled in the Amazon, the Andes and the historically rich north.

I changed from a life of not feeling like I belonged anywhere to feeling that I belonged everywhere as long as I had myself. So when I left Peru, I decided it was time to grow permanent roots, ground myself and give up my nomadic life. I settled into a little house in Brisbane, where, unlike in Sydney, where I would have been held hostage to an enormous mortgage for a small apartment in an anonymous high-rise, I was able to buy a lovely cottage in a neighbourhood community where we support each other but don't live in each other's pockets. I still travel, but now I have a place that centres me, that I can return to after I have expanded.

As for marrying again? I haven't, and I likely never will. I love my life as it is. Maybe it was the realisation that my grandmother, who started to assemble my dowry when I turned twelve, and who had stated over and over again that it was important to get married and that married women always had to walk the lower path, proclaimed one thing as truth, while living another. Her husband had suddenly died at the age of forty-seven, and she single-handedly had to raise two young sons in post-war Germany. After my father and his brother had started their own families, she lived happily and contentedly by herself until she died peacefully in her bed, just as she had predicted, at the age of eighty-six.

Her example helped me realise that even when you think you are following crucial social rules, you can make up your own. At any time in your life.

Angela Heise *is a human skills and leadership coach with nearly thirty years of experience. She helps women take back their time, confidence, and purpose.*

Even though she'd done a lot of personal growth work before her marriage, Angela found herself falling into old generational patterns, which led her to put her own dreams and goals aside. At forty, after her divorce, she rebooted her life on her own terms and in a way that felt true to herself. Angela knows firsthand how hard it can be to break old habits and beliefs and see new possibilities. Before pausing her ambitions during marriage, she'd built a diverse career in media production, event organising and general management, living in nine countries and working in sixteen.

Angela's personal work and professional experience inspired Emotional Productivity®, *a framework that helps people manage emotions, needs, and boundaries for healthy, drama-free relationships. Today, Angela supports women over forty to put themselves first and show them that reinvention is possible and rewarding.*

Things I Wish I'd Known When I Was Younger

Hannah Babbington

One of the benefits of aging – and there are a few – is that it provides us with the perspective to reflect on our lives thus far and understand where we've come from and how we got here. In our teens and early twenties, we often feel invincible; confident we can achieve anything we set our minds to. However, as we age and life starts to throw challenges our way, we come to realise that we are in fact mere mortals and that perhaps it may not be quite as easy as we thought to achieve the dreams and aspirations we held from our younger years.

Beginning my journey into my forties, there are a few key lessons I've learned up to this point. I've no doubt there will be even more realisations in my fifties – and beyond. The point is that I'm excited to see where life takes me and what lessons I'll learn along the way.

Here's the lowdown so far ...

Only Compete Against Yourself

I'm an identical twin and I'm convinced that this is part of the reason I'm such a competitive person. As humans, it's natural to compare ourselves to others. We wish we had the perfect family or the newest car just like so-and-so. We set ourselves an impossible checklist of tasks to complete by a certain age: I must be married by twenty-five, have three kids by the age of thirty and be at the peak of my career.

As we get older, however, I think it becomes more apparent that we're all just doing our best to juggle life's seemingly endless demands. Of course, we can have a rough idea of how we want our life to pan out, but this shouldn't involve trying to be better than everyone else.

I married at thirty-four. I've recently obtained my Bachelor of Science – at forty-one – and I'm far from being at the peak of my career. But I'm happy. I drive a twelve-year-old Ford Fiesta, buy my clothes at sales and live well below my means. I'm certainly not trying to 'keep up with the Joneses' because that would be exhausting and unfulfilling.

If you're worried how this makes you look, take note of my next lesson.

No-one Cares

I'm not being mean. This is meant to be positive. Let me explain why.

On my twenty-seventh birthday, I hopped on a plane to Australia. (I was born in England and chose to make the beautiful land down under my home several years ago.) At the time, I was single. I'd taken a redundancy payout from my job and decided to spend the money backpacking in a foreign land. When I walked into my first hostel in Sydney, I was greeted by hordes of super-slim, young and gorgeous women who were doing the same thing as me. I immediately felt out of my depth. I wondered how I could possibly put on a bikini and strut around Bondi Beach without strangers pointing and staring at my cellulite, wobbly bits and hairy knees.

After several months travelling up the east coast, I finally arrived in Cairns. This place changed me. Something just clicked. I realised that everyone was focused on themselves about ninety per cent of the time. No-one was holding a magnifying glass and checking every little flaw on my body. Everyone was there, enjoying the beautiful, carefree lifestyle and rocking their swimwear – whatever their size and shape.

This was a revelation to me – no-one cares.

No-one cares if you forget to shave your knees. No-one cares if your bum wobbles when you walk. No-one cares if you have stretchmarks on your stomach.

So, what did I do?

I bought a bikini and wore it – the first time ever – at the beach. (Well, it was a lagoon. If you've been to Cairns, you'll remember the crocodile warnings at the beach!) At twenty-seven years of age, I was finally wearing a bikini in public because NO-ONE CARES!

This obsession with perfection leads me to my next little truth nugget ...

Failure IS an Option

As women, we are constantly placing a huge amount of pressure on ourselves. We strive to be successful in business. We want to be the best parent to our kids and maintain the perfect household while balancing all the challenges that life inevitably throws at us. Did you ever stop to think what would happen if you did drop the ball on something? Would the Earth stop spinning? Would life as you know it come to a crashing halt? Of course it wouldn't. In fact, when we fail at something, it gives us the opportunity to go deeper.

I failed my driving test four times.

During my first test, the examiner asked me to turn right from a one-way street and I realised I was in the left-hand lane. Instantly, I knew I'd failed as this constituted a major fault. I burst into floods of tears and the poor examiner had to walk back to the test centre – just five minutes into my test – to fetch my instructor as I was too fraught to continue driving.

I failed the next one too, but at least I finished that one.

Then I failed again.

When I finally passed on my fourth test, I was absolutely over the moon.

And do you know what? I'm a pretty good driver now. The important thing was that I didn't give up.

Similarly, I dropped out of university when I was eighteen years old. I managed the first three months before realising it wasn't for me. I left under a bit of a cloud – and with a sizeable chunk of student debt. In my twenties, I attempted it again through the Open University. While the course itself was great, I ended up dropping out after a year to go travelling.

Fast-forward to the age of thirty-four and I finally picked up my studies again just a few weeks after getting married. I finally graduated this year, at the age of forty-one, with a degree in Astronomical and Space Studies from the University of Southern Queensland.

There is so much we can do in this life, but we must not be scared to fail, or we risk missing out on incredible opportunities. It is these opportunities that may become our legacy.

Indeed, failure is not in the falling down but in the staying down.

You Won't Be Remembered for Long

This is a sensitive subject for many. The realisation came to me fairly recently and I'm still processing what it means for me.

I've known forever that I don't want children. There was no specific reason, and I definitely don't hate kids; I just never wanted to have any of my own. This leads to the age-old question: Who will continue your legacy?

But let's be realistic for a second – the majority of us know the names of our parents and grandparents, but who remembers the names of their great grandparents and great great grandparents? I would guess that very few of us do, and thus, having children is perhaps not the 'be all and end all' of leaving a legacy.

Once I came to this realisation, I suddenly felt there was a lot more meaning to my life. I saw that I could choose other ways to be remembered.

From a young age, my dad was sick with Hodgkin's Lymphoma. It came back many times until he passed away when I was twenty-one. He always knew he wouldn't 'make old bones' – his words – and he wanted to leave a legacy. He wanted to be remembered long after he'd left this world, so he wrote a book, got it published and was incredibly proud of it. The book was called *Thundersley: A Pictorial History* and is a postcard collection of the village where I grew up. Everyone I knew in the village owned at least one copy and it sat proudly in our school library. Even now, more than thirty years after it was written, people still talk about it. I just know my dad would love to hear that.

Sometimes people ask who will take care of me when I'm elderly if I don't have children? Another way to leave a legacy is to serve others less fortunate. I used to take my beautiful greyhound, Murphy, to an aged care home once a week to volunteer as a therapy dog. Almost all the residents living there had families, yet I saw very few of them visiting. The harsh reality is that having children offers absolutely no guarantee of being looked after by them when you're old.

The point I'm trying to make here is that if you want to leave a legacy, but you don't have kids, don't panic. There are many ways to be remembered and one of the best is to be authentic to yourself – even if you think it makes you a little bit weird.

Be Your Weird, Awkward Little Self

Life is short. Very short.

Once I hit forty, this seemed to become even more evident. Adding to my understanding that no-one cares, I decided that life is far too short to be concerned with how others perceive me. I'll admit that I'm a little bit weird and awkward but being an identical twin and growing up in a small village in England automatically made me a little bit weird. We were often referred to as 'The Twinnies' at school and one child even asked us once why we didn't get the same school report because 'you're basically the same person'.

My hobbies are also a little strange – I love astronomy, cloud-watching and plane-spotting. I constantly have a stiff neck from always looking up!

When I was at school, I really enjoyed birdwatching with my dad, and I subscribed to an ornithology magazine called *BirdLife*. On one occasion, a boy in my class found a copy and everyone had a good laugh. It didn't put me off, though, because that's who I am and that's what I liked doing.

So please ... do what you love and do it as often as you can because before you know it, there's no time left.

Be Kind

There's a saying that 'people won't remember what you said or did, but they will remember how you made them feel'. So, while you're busy not caring what anyone thinks and being your awkward, weird little self, remember to spread some kindness. Compliment someone on their outfit. Check in with the new person on their first day at work. Help someone take their shopping to their car. Even the smallest acts of kindness can have the biggest impact on someone's life.

We all have a different journey. Some will face more challenges than others. I was fortunate to grow up in a close family with my mum, dad and two sisters. My dad was ill for much of my childhood, but I have beautiful memories of our summer holidays together, filled with so much love and laughter.

After my wonderful dad passed away, I realised my family now comprised of magnificently strong and inspiring women. My nan lived independently in her own home until she passed away at the grand age of ninety-two. She was a truly incredible woman who overcame terrible tragedy, outliving her husband and both her children, but she always found something to be positive about. My mum has also shaped my life, teaching me to be generous and to give to others. My sisters constantly leave me in awe with their career achievements and kindness towards those less fortunate than themselves.

I hope some of this may resonate with you too because life is short.

Have fun! Forget about out wrinkles. Proudly and confidently be yourself.

(Dedicated to the awesome women in my life: Pat, Hilda, Lucie and Emma xx)

Hannah Babbington *grew up in a small village in the UK called Thundersley with her mum, dad, older sister Emma and identical twin Lucie. She loved school and was always a high achiever. At the age of eighteen, Hannah went to university but dropped out after the first term, realising it was too much for her to be away from home. When she was twenty-one, her dad passed away after years of being sick. This was a defining moment in Hannah's life, and she suddenly became a little bit braver. At twenty-seven, Hannah left England to backpack around Australia. She ended up meeting her future husband and ha now lived in Melbourne for almost eleven years. After getting married at thirty-four, Hannah finally went back to university and graduated this year – at the age of forty-one – with a Bachelor of Science, with Distinction in Astronomical and Space Sciences. Hannah loves astronomy, sunrises, adopting dogs (currently two greyhounds) and spending time in her community.*

Resilience, Renewal and Reinvention

The Tassie Move

Lee-Anne Kendall

One day, as I sat on the same grey couch, in the same three-bedroom house I'd rented for the last seven years in Perth, Western Australia, I realised I wanted something else. I wasn't sure what it was, but I was ready to find out.

Twelve months earlier, on my thirty-eighth birthday in 2017, I'd become a women's life coach. Since then, I'd been making subtle changes here and there, but I still felt like something was missing.

I tried to shake the feeling off and be happy with where I was, but when my daughter came home from school one day, absolutely devastated because her so-called best friend was fighting with her and had tried to have a bunch of girls beat her up, that feeling came back stronger than ever.

I blurted out, "Do you want to move to Tassie?" I don't know why I said it; I'd always loved the look of Tasmania and we were well over the heat here in Perth – forty-degree summer days, anyone? – but surely that was a rash thing to say?

To my surprise, my daughter said, "If you can get a job, yes, I'll move to Tassie."

The seed was planted. If I could get a job, then we'd go! That's how quickly things happen sometimes.

I'd actually thought about moving to Tasmania on and off for around four years but now the thought wouldn't let go. It was constant. Then, the next week at work, I was looking through the regular Repco newsletter. On the back page was the 'Internal Positions Vacant' section and there it was – a position in Hobart for a parts person. *[Insert shocked look on face.]*

I stayed calm but inside I was jumping for joy and tingling all over! This was THE sign that shit was about to get real.

That night, I showed my daughter the newsletter. "The Universe has said yes to us doing this," I said.

She rolled her eyes. "You know I don't believe in any of that crap," she said, "but yes, let's do it. There's nothing keeping me here and a change could be good."

Admittedly, that view made me sad for her – but excited for us. This place was her home. She'd grown up here since she was nine. It was home for me too, so it was going to be very weird to move somewhere new. Anyway, I still had to get the job and told myself to snap out of it.

I waited till Monday afternoon before I stopped being nervous long enough to ring the Hobart branch and talk to the manager about the job and the possibility of getting a transfer from Rockingham to Hobart. To my delight, he was interested – but he had to talk to my current boss so he could see if I was a good fit for the team.

"I'll ring you back by next Monday to let you know," he said. The other thing he said was that I'd need to find accommodation – but it would be hard because there were people living in tents at the showgrounds. I had a bit of a chuckle, thinking he was joking, but he wasn't. "It's not a joke," he said. "I'm serious. There's a real housing crisis going on here in Hobart."

I'd deal with that later. For now, I had to let my current boss know I was looking at transferring and to expect a phone call from the manager in Hobart. I went to his office and had the chat, and he said he was happy for me and would definitely give permission for the transfer if requested.

So far, so good.

That night I Googled Tassie pictures and created an affirmation screensaver for my phone. It was a photo of Dove Lake on Cradle Mountain with the words 'I fucking did it. I manifested Tassie!' That was the thing I saw first, every single time I looked at my phone.

I started to get super excited – but when I hadn't heard back from the Hobart manager by the following Wednesday, I started to doubt this was going to happen. I waited until the Friday and finally rang him, but he was busy, and I was told to try him again later in the day. I tried again twice but no luck. The same with the next day. The assistant manager said he'd have him ring me back as it was important, so I just had to wait.

I'm really not good with the whole waiting game.

I tried to distract myself with other shit. I also knew that with the Law of Attraction, you have to let the Universe know you're serious, so I found some boxes and started packing my big built-in robes, thinking this would make him ring me.

It didn't work.

The next day. I was all choked up with a head cold and feeling pretty sorry for myself. I remember saying out loud to the Universe, " I'm going to leave it in your hands. If this is meant to be, it will happen. I'm going to sleep."

Four hours later, I woke up to a missed call!

I rang him back. "You have the job," he said. "You'll start at the beginning of August."

This only left me two months to get my shit sorted and be there – and that's when I began to panic! Two months! How the hell was I going to do this?

I started writing a list of everything I needed to do, and another list of what we needed to take with us. By the time I'd finished, I had pages of things to do and very little time to do it!

The first step was telling our landlords that we were leaving. Luckily, they were my friend Stephanie's parents, and we'd been there for seven years, so they were lovely about it. They just asked me if I had any suggestions for anybody who could move in after we left. My friend Wendy came to mind. She'd been wanting to leave her marriage, so this was the perfect opportunity for her. She loved the idea and met with my landlords a week later to discuss everything. Wendy was also happy to keep our pets in the house, so that was a relief.

Now, everything was starting to feel real.

Next up was accommodation.

I went onto Facebook to look for accommodation groups in Tassie. I messaged a guy called Matthew about a place and explained my situation. Once again the Universe did something amazing – the owners of the house were coming to Perth for a holiday, so we arranged to meet for a coffee and a chat. Everything was just falling into place. At our meeting, they gave me all the paperwork to fill out and said they were happy to rent to us. We could even have all of our fur babies at the property. "We just had to give notice to our current tenant," they said. "Sixty days."

I was so excited.

My start date for my new job would be the 18th of August. I had somewhere to live and it turned out that Glenorchy – where the place was situated – was not too far from the branch. The owners had a fair bit of work to do to get the house into shape but said it would be ready for us to move in by the time I started work, if not just before.

It was now June. That gave me a couple of months. I knew I could do this.

The next job on my list was to tell family and friends I was leaving. This was hard. So many people said I was crazy moving to a place I'd never been before, where I knew no-one. "It's just what I'm doing," I said. "There's something about Tassie that's calling me." My workmates, on the other hand, were shocked but also excited for me.

The next couple of months seemed to fly by. With the packing, cleaning, decluttering, donating, selling, getting rid of shit – while still working – it was all a bit of a blur.

There was so much to do and so little time left.

My last day at work arrived. They had a going away thing for me and gave me a handmade clock that had the number eleven on every space, instead of the normal numbers. I was so blown away by the gesture. I'd always said it was 11.11 on my shifts and they'd all become used to me doing angel numbers. It was sweet and personal – I still have it in my office. They also serviced my car and left me a little 'drive safe' note on my windscreen; it made me smile every time I got in the car.

Wendy came over a couple of days later to pick up Tash, our dog. She was going to look after her for us while we did our trip. This was awesome because it meant she was still in the same house until she was be sent over later, once we were settled along with our three cats, Ash, Mash and Lola. I'd already researched prices and what I had to do for this to happen with JetPets. I bawled my eyes out saying goodbye to

Tash as I wouldn't see her again for a few months. She didn't have a clue what was happening, and I don't think she really cared.

After Tash was gone, I stopped and looked around. We were leaving in a couple of days and I still had so much to do. We were only taking the IX35, which was a very small SUV, and could only take what we could fit. I didn't have time to go back to the op shop again and there was so much stuff left in the house. I didn't know how I was going to get it all done!

Just then, my old next-door neighbour came over and asked how it was all going and if we were ready to go. I told her I still had a pile of stuff in the bottom loungeroom to get rid of as it hadn't all sold on the marketplace. Jackie said she'd take it all and sell it later. I couldn't believe it; she was a godsend. The next minute, she had her Pajero backed up to the front door and we were loading it all in.

Done. All gone. Now I could breathe a little.

Lauren – my best friend of over twenty-five years – came to say goodbye the next day. It was lovely to see her before I left, particularly as we weren't sure she'd make it. But she made the drive from all the way north of the river to Rockingham. To be honest, I was worried about leaving her because she was in a crap relationship that had taken the shine out of her eyes and I wasn't going to be her safe place anymore once I left. That scared me a lot.

I kept telling her she could visit and call me anytime. Waving as she drove down the road was hard. It started to really hit me then that I was going. I was terrified. This was a big thing. No, scratch that; it was a HUGE thing. I was going to be driving from one side of Australia to the other – 4500 km, give or take.

Was I as crazy as people were telling me?

Two days before we were due to leave, the owner of the house messaged me with a massive bombshell! The house had been trashed and they were no longer going to rent it. Due to all the damage, they'd decided to sell it instead. I actually thought they were joking at first, but they weren't. What was I going to do? We were leaving in a couple of days. I'd sold all my stuff. I had Wendy moving in. My new boss was expecting me.

All of that and we had no house to move into!

So many things were swirling in my mind at that moment! Maybe it was a sign from the Universe that I wasn't meant to go. Was I really going to be living in a tent at the showgrounds like my new boss said? I couldn't not go after all this ... could I?

I sat on my air mattress in absolute shock. Then, a couple of hours later, I shook it all off and started packing the car. We just had to do it!

That night, I don't think I slept at all.

The next morning, moving day was here at last! I'd packed most of the car the night before but still had quite a lot left to do. Suitcases in, air beds down, blankets and pillows in vacuum-sealed bags ... everywhere I looked, I kept finding more and more. I was running out of room and time fast. We had to get on the road for the ten-hour drive to our first stop at Esperance. I was tired from no sleep and my daughter kept asking questions and telling me stuff I already knew, like 'that won't fit in there,' and 'we still have such-and-such to pack,' and eventually I lost the plot. Yelling at nothing, I was throwing shit out of the car with tears streaming down my face; it had finally all caught up with me. The last three months ... I was exhausted. My brain couldn't handle anymore; I was done.

When I'd calmed down, my daughter said, "Why don't we just go tomorrow? We don't have to go today."

Just like that – she made so much sense. I messaged my cousin, saying 'one more day' – she was fine with that. Then we slowly unpacked some of the car, rearranging things so they'd fit better.

The next morning, we put the final couple of things in the car – and we left. It was so easy. We stopped by my good friend's house. Michelle made us breakfast and fluffy coffee. We had photos and hugs with her and her daughter and shed lots of tears. Michelle had been a constant in my life; I was going to miss her heaps. We used to catch up for coffee once a fortnight and laugh so much. It was hard to imagine this wouldn't be a thing anymore.

Then, finally, we were on the road. On our way. Goodbye, Rockingham. Goodbye, Perth.

We stayed in my hometown, Esperance, for the next week. I'd left and gone to Queensland when I was eighteen, but my brother Chook and other family still lived here. My cousin Fabianne was lovely enough to put us up. The entire time we were there, I was applying for houses left, right and centre. At one point, an owner actually contacted me himself, asked me some questions and said he'd let me know for sure the following week. "But, you've pretty much got the house," he said.

It was such a relief … but we still had to wait for confirmation.

I also had to book the *Spirit of Tasmania* from Melbourne to Tasmania. As it turned out, owing to the fact that, in winter, they only have one boat going while the other's in maintenance, we couldn't get a car spot on the ferry until the thirteenth, which was over two weeks away – and the day I was meant to start work.

Once again, there was a spanner in the works.

I had no choice but to call my new boss and let him know that I wouldn't be able to start until a week after the proposed date. He wasn't happy but said, "It is what it is, I guess."

On the way across the Nullarbor, we stopped at Eucla and went for a fifteen-minute drive down the road to see the Cliffs. It was pretty insane and made me tear up; we were on the edge of Australia.

Then – I received notification we hadn't been approved for the house after all.

We were still homeless.

The next day, we made it to the border of South Australia and Western Australia. We took photos at the sign, as you do. Not long after, we saw a sign saying Head Of Bight Whale Watching. I looked at my daughter. "Why not?" we both said and pulled in.

It was huge! There were cars and buses everywhere. I had no clue this place existed! We paid our entry fee and walked around for a bit, then went outside to these zig-zag platforms that seemed to go forever … and then I saw them! WHALES! There were four or five of them, although I couldn't tell for sure so I just started running to the end, I was so excited to see actual whales in the ocean in front of my very own eyes! They were still quite far out but, at the same time, they felt so close. It was magnificent seeing them gliding through the water.

Once we got over the awe of what we just witnessed, we were on our way – heading to Ceduna. We nearly ran out of petrol because of our detour and the fact there were no petrol stops along the way. For the last fifty kilometres, I was shitting myself as I watched the fuel gauge go down, kilometre by kilometre. I was trying not to show my daughter how stressed out I was, but all I could think about was getting stranded out here in the middle of nowhere! You hear stories all the time – people dying of thirst or going missing because they walked away from their car and it was so bloody hot outside.

Finally, I saw a sign – Ceduna 11 kms. I had fourteen kilometres in my tank, so I was banking on this being correct. We pulled into the service station with four kilometres left in the petrol tank! I knew Nan and Pop were watching over us then, to make sure we were safe.

Our next stop was Streaky Bay in South Australia. We got a cabin on the beach for a couple of days and were woken the next morning by a pelican outside our door. Seeing it was a surprise, and it actually stayed at our cabin, on and off, during our whole stay. We also checked out The Blowholes. It's really cool how the waves create noises in the rocks.

Over the next few days, we travelled through South Australia. We made it to the halfway point in Kimba and saw 'the big cockatoo'.

Driving along the A8, now in Victoria, we wondered about the mountains in the distance. After Googling, we found out they were The Grampians. The scenery at our hotel was breathtaking; I'd never stayed in a place so pretty before.

After being on the open roads for a couple of weeks, we arrived in Melbourne. Compared to where we'd come from, it was hectic and driving in the city was insane. Who invented those hook turn things?

This 4,500 km trip had definitely tested my patience more than once. It was the longest distance I'd ever driven before but it was nearly over. We were so close to the finish line.

The ferry was way bigger than I expected. As I pulled into our allocated spot, the reality that we would finally be in Tasmania tomorrow was starting to hit me. I was excited and scared – both at the same time. We went to the cabin – which was extremely basic – to settle in and then had a bit of a look around before dinner. It was so pretty looking at the lights of Melbourne as we pulled out of port.

The next few weeks were a whirlwind – travelling to Hobart, meeting my new boss in person, learning about my new store and applying for houses. Luckily, the Discovery Caravan Park gave us permission to stay in one of their one-bedroom self-contained cabins for a couple of weeks. It was soo nice to be able to stay in the same place for a while and, as a bonus, it was only twenty minutes from work.

I was still also looking for a place to rent. Some of the places I saw were really bad – full of mould, dingy, rotting wood – yet they wanted

$400 a week for them. I worried we were never going to find anything. Money was getting really tight and I realised I could only afford to stay one more week at the caravan park. I joined a group on Facebook called *That's it I'm moving to Tassie* and posted that we were looking for a place. A lady reached out and said she'd just bought a place but was on the mainland for the next four months so we could rent it for that time at least. However, we couldn't move in for a fortnight.

The next day, my boss asked me how I was going. I just broke down in tears. "I've got no money left. We can only stay in the park until the end of the week and I can't get the house for two."

He was so nice about it. "I'll lend you the money for a week's rent at the caravan park," he said. I barely knew this man and he was going to help me!

Being a single mum for seventeen years, I was so used to having to do everything for myself, it made me cry even more. I gave him the biggest hug and apologised for crying all over him.

We got the keys for the house in Lindisfarne on my birthday. There was no gas bottle, and we couldn't get one ordered for another two days, so it was freezing inside and we couldn't cook unless it was microwaved – but we had somewhere to stay.

The next four months flew by. I'd started applying for houses around month two and once again was having no luck. With days before we had to move out, I messaged the real estate agent that we rented this house through and asked if they had anything available. It turned out they did – but it was $560 a week and no pets. I had no choice; I had to take it. The house was old, but it was big and the view was gorgeous with mountains right outside our window.

The no pets rule meant I couldn't get my fur babies over from WA. In the end, Tash had to be rehoused – with a lovely lady. Ash was also rehomed, but sadly Lola ran away and Mash died. It was so hard knowing I'd never see them again.

My daughter started a Tafe course and we'd both started to make some friends. I loved my job and my colleagues made both of feel like family. For my fortieth birthday, they all chipped to bring my mum over from Western Australia for two weeks. I hadn't seen her in person for five years! It the best present.

The rent was tough. After about four months, we were literally living on $50 after all the bills. I was drowning in debt, my car payments were behind and they were talking repossession, so I had to start working six days a week just so we could breathe a little. It was tiring and, twelve months later, I was back doing the 'searching for a rental' dance. With some help from my boss, we finally moved to a place on Midway Point with water views. Getting up every morning, sitting on the balcony and looking at the insane view with my coffee – you couldn't beat it.

While we were living at Midway Point, I was promoted to sales representative after my boss left. I also got a pay rise, which was really nice, along with a company car. More importantly, I could finally start looking into buying my own house; the only issue was the house prices in Hobart were beyond my means. I ended up applying for a house in East Devonport and crossed my fingers. As luck would have it, I met the manager of the Devonport branch and found out that he had a position vacant at his store. I asked if I could have that position – and the next week he rang to say I could have the position. I'd thought that the house sale was a sure thing – but apparently it had fallen through, and the bank said no.

Once again, I was on Facebook, begging.

Once again, the Universe seemed to hear and I ended up being offered a little cottage to rent.

I started work at the Devonport store. The crew were nice enough but it was definitely a lot quieter than the Hobart store. I only lasted a couple of months before I started applying for other jobs. There was one I really liked the sound of. It was in employment services but I hadn't worked in the industry for years, so I didn't really know how good my chances were. I went home that night and applied for it – and then did some scripting in my journal saying that I had the job and was loving it.

Four weeks went by and I assumed I hadn't got the position when, out of the blue, the manager rang to invite me in for an interview. I got the job!

A couple of years went by, and I found myself on the rental merry-go-round again so decided to try applying to buy. I had a better income now – and job stability – and after speaking to a mortgage broker, decided to try for the MyHome program. I had to clear up some bills beforehand, and make a few sacrifices, including selling my little blue baby – the car that had brought us over here – but once I did, I was ready.

This time felt totally different. It was calm rather than anxiety-inducing and stressful. We missed out on the first house we wanted, then a house around the corner from that one came up. There'd been no offers on it. It was old and dated, but the kitchen and bathroom had been renovated, and it had a large yard, a good feel and a beach at the end of the street. We put our offer in and ... it was accepted!

On the 20th of November 2023, I took possession of my very own house. I bawled my eyes out! After twenty years being a single mum – the stress and struggling of renting and everything else that had happened – I just let it all out.

Moving to Tassie had been worth it.

Lee-Anne Kendall *is a women's life coach who draws on her own life experiences to empower women to heal from the past, rediscover their self-worth and create lasting change. As a single parent for nearly twenty-four years, a survivor of domestic violence and someone who overcame addiction, Lee-Anne knows firsthand the power of resilience and transformation. Having completely reinvented her life – moving across Australia and building a new path – she now helps other women do the same, teaching manifestation and the Universal Laws as tools for creating a life you love. Lee-Anne is also a certified Emotional Freedom Technique (tapping) practitioner, a Law of Attraction practitioner and is currently completing her Masters in neuro-linguistic programming. She runs the Empowered AF Woman 365 community on Facebook, offers intuitive oracle card readings and continues to inspire women worldwide.*

Bob O'clock

Alice Monaghan

In June 2015, at thirty-three years old, I became a widow and a sole parent to my three children, all under five years old. I was relieved my husband had died but also totally and utterly devastated. One of the greatest things I've learned is that there is no 'normal' when you're grieving, but everything you do feel while you're grieving is completely normal.

We met at work, in Western Australia, in 2008. Bob was enigmatic; a ball of boundless energy who lit up any room he walked into. He was tall, he was loud and he was proud. He naturally drew people in, effortlessly encouraging the most miserable people to laugh and instilling confidence in those who were the most insecure. Bob moved through life with ease. He never seemed to get bogged down in the stress of work or the injustices in the world. He simply bubbled over any issues that life threw his way and carried others along with him for the ride. Nothing was too hard or overwhelming. Bob saw the bright side of every situation and – he absolutely adored me.

Our attraction to each other was magnetic. We were fascinated with each other, the conversation never ran dry, we had a similar sense of humour, the air was electric when we were together and we both started thinking that we couldn't imagine life without each other. We had a major problem though; we were both in relationships with other people. We decided that we didn't want our future to be marred by any impulsive infidelities, so we both separated from our partners before giving our own relationship a chance.

Bob showered me with affection and the way he threw himself at life was something I had never experience before, I was drawn to him like a moth to a flame. I wasn't alone in my attraction to him, everyone adored him. And he adored everyone, but I was special. He doted on me with his infinite enthusiasm. He would cook me breakfast, lunch and dinner without hesitation, always checked to see if I had everything I wanted and made me endless cups of tea.

Bob's zest for life made him shine and radiate joy. He was one of those people who enriched your life just by being in the room with you, he was someone who deserved to have things named after them, and therefore, Bob had been affectionately assigned a specific time of day by his work colleagues and friends, just to celebrate him - 8.08 – BOB O'clock.

In return for his dedication to me, I provided him a safe environment to be himself, a stable, calm demeanour that allowed him the space to be BIG, never asking him to temper his energy levels, never restricting his need to escape on his push bikes, never asking him to slow down. If he wasn't at home or work, he would be riding through the streets on his fixed-gear roadie or pummelling himself through the bush on his mountain bike. I loved his energy and it filled me with a sense of peace to see how happy he was. However, this was also no mean feat on my behalf, allowing him this unbridled freedom to escape whenever he needed to, was fraught with consequence. There was a reason why his friends nicknamed him 'Bubble Wrap Bobby', he was constantly injured on mountain bike trails due to his unwavering addiction to the thrill of pushing his body to its limits. We never could have foreseen that this drive to live on the edge, would eventually be his undoing and rather than admonish him for his lack of responsibility to himself and his physical welfare, these things made me love him even more deeply. He was the extroverted yin to my introverted yang. While he was the centre of attention, I could be free to enjoy the ambience, releasing my inner party animal as the drinks flowed. Bob and I lived together, worked together and played together and we could not have been happier.

Alcohol featured heavily in our lives, which never seemed a problem, as there was always good company and always reasons to celebrate. We were married quickly. It was an auspicious date, the 9.09.09 - 9 months exactly from the day of our first date, it was a Wednesday wedding and it rained, which was also espoused to be 'lucky'. And, as luck would have it, we fell pregnant a couple of months later, but little did we know what was in store for us.

Unfortunately, our first pregnancy became the catalyst for a plethora of challenges. Bob lost his job a week prior to us finding out about our pregnancy, he became concerned about providing for his family, the anxiety heightened when he started a new job, but he settled quickly and he continued to love his life and the people in it. Bob always said that he lived life 'to the max times ten' and that he had the enthusiasm of a '6-year-old boy in a grown man's body'. His energy and exuberance defined him. He would push his drinking, his riding and his joy for life to the max, and that was just, Bob.

The first cracks in our relationship began to show when Bob's fervour for the party life continued its intensity, despite the pregnancy and my need for more rest and my inability to participate in the alcohol consumption. His attention to me and my new maternal needs began to wane when he became drunk and my own resentment started to creep in. I needed him more, but he was giving me less.

When I was pregnant, we found out that our daughter would be born with gastroschisis, a birth defect that is defined by the baby's intestines and other organs protruding through a hole in the abdominal wall. Bob and I became closer with the joint concern for her wellbeing, and Bob's focus returned to his family. Our lives became a series of medical appointments, scans and updating friends, family and work colleagues on her progress. Our lives became the focus of everyone's attention; the world revolved around us. The fear that Bob and I shared over potential pregnancy complications and risks of our daughter's permanent disability or death drove much of our emotional connection throughout the pregnancy. Bob would escape to the bush on his mountain bike regularly to release his stress, and I could appreciate his absences as a necessary time for him to regroup and return to me with more energy and a renewed sense of duty.

Louise was born in winter, 2010. She was our 'Warrior Princess', requiring a two-week hospital stay and very little intervention, she came home on my 29th birthday and never skipped a beat. However, our sigh of relief and excitement was marred once again by Bob losing his job. Again he lamented his ability to provide a stable financial environment for his family, again he suffered damage to his self-esteem. Again, he bounced back and into another role, this time, as Assistant Function Manager at one of the most prestigious restaurants in Perth. Finally, he was flying high on the renewed sense of self-importance and income that his new position provided him.

Our marriage ticked along as well as most relationships after the introduction of a tiny bundle of screams and dimples. We bickered over whose turn it was to get up in the middle of the night, who was the most tired and who had changed the most nappies. Bob started spending more and more time at work, and I spent more and more time alone.

Over time, Bob started becoming frustrated with his new role, he was making mistakes and his position was under review. He was again dismissed from his job, just as we found out that we were pregnant with our son, Patrick. We had been discussing moving back to Queensland, and it seemed the perfect time to make the move.

We arrived in Queensland in January 2012. Initially, Bob was excited about being in a new city, with so much potential to find new friends and bike trails. He was reluctant to find work, and as his alcohol consumption increased, my trust in his ability to independently care for our 18-month-old daughter was tested, so I rarely left him alone with her.

I began to wonder if the figurative '6-year-old boy in a grown man's body' was, in fact, who I was married to.

Patrick was born in winter, 2012. Bobby's bonny baby boy; My clingy, refluxy, spew machine. He was 9lb 9oz at birth and guzzled milk like there was nothing else important in life. He wanted to be held constantly. If I put him down, he cried or spewed. I slept upright on the couch with him for 3 months straight. It was an exhausting start to life with two children. Somehow between the birth of Louise and the birth of Patrick, I had evolved an ever-growing fear of leaving the house. Going back to full-time work seemed like an infinitesimal stretch of my will power, so I never did. I would later recognise this as post-natal depression.

Bob struggled to find anything satisfying in the new city and ricocheted from one casual job to another, never really settling on anything that was stable. He struggled to regain his passion and energy for life, but he still had his passion for me and for our babies. He doted on us all within the home, ensuring our needs were met.

Bob's drinking during this time was moderate and for the most part, we enjoyed each other's company. We learned to live within our means and found some kind of rigour for the humdrum of life with young children. Our ability to overcome the little challenges that life kept throwing at us, continued to bring us together, albeit, with a little less patience, and with some added resentment. I resented his lack of desire for full-time work, and he simply mirrored that resentment back at me. Neither of us felt obligated to be the bread winner, however, where I was cutting back on spending, he was increasing it with his desire to consume alcohol. We considered these issues 'things that will go away with time as the kids grow and we have more freedom to each go out and work', and we were soon pregnant again with our third and last baby.

Before I knew what hit me, Bob's desire to push his body to the limit had returned, but the positivity had left him. He was suddenly out on his bike, in parks, drinking all day. He would leave home early and come home late. He had a casual job that paid cash, and I barely saw a dollar. I cried on the phone as I organised shopping vouchers from the Salvation Army, and with one child on my back and the other on my hip, picked up free boxes of food from Lifeline as my belly grew. Our government benefit barely covered our rent and his casual work income was a liquid luxury, limited to Bob. He was oblivious to his drain on the life we had planned, but he also continued to dote on me when he was home and drunk. I found the dichotomy of attitudes to his family life difficult to reconcile in my brain.

One night in March 2014, I woke to Patrick crying. Bob and I were sleeping separately due to Bob's snoring, and I found that Patrick had crawled into Bob's bed. He was crushing him and was millimetres from smothering Patrick with his shoulder. I woke Bobby by smacking him in the face, he was far too drunk to hear me, and he was, at that stage, far too cumbersome for me to roll him away to save my boy. I told Bob that he needed to move out and get help. He left for rehab two days later. It was that moment that I realised that the light of my world, the person upon which the axis of my world spun, had somehow, right under my nose, become an alcoholic.

Bob was granted a three-month stay in a rehab facility 1.5hrs from where we lived. I was three months away from giving birth to our third child, a baby girl. I found support in weekly Al Anon meetings during that time and learned how to 'detach with love'. Regular calls from Bob reinvigorated our love for each other, and I began to find hope that we would be able to get through it all with our deep friendship intact. I established routines with the kids and pushed through the pain of pelvic separation until it became too difficult for me to bath the kids or even roll over in bed. I asked Bob to come home early, he was doing so well and we both had faith that he could continue to work on his sobriety at home.

I had contacted his close friend, Cameron* and asked if he could pick Bob up from his accommodation and bring him home, as I didn't feel that I was up for a three-hour round trip with my pelvis threatening to split in two with every movement I made. Cameron happily obliged, however, asking Cameron to undertake this task might have been the biggest mistake I had made to date.

Bob arrived home to me, stoned.

I couldn't believe it. I looked at Cameron, and then at Bob, neither realising just how stupid it is to offer drugs to someone returning from rehab. Any hope that I had for Bob's sobriety and in turn, our relationship, disappeared that day.

I reminded myself of the vows that Bob and I had shared at our wedding; 'through sickness and in health'. I'd reassured myself that I had been there for Bob while he was sick, I struggled alone with two toddlers while heavily pregnant and suffering pelvic separation while he was in rehab, receiving three square meals a day and daily massages. I made a pact with myself, if Bob wasn't there for me during my 6-week recovery from my imminent c-section, then I would walk away from the relationship. I refused to be a doormat for an alcoholic; regardless how much I loved them.

Bob started drinking again before I even gave birth. "I didn't get to finish the full three months, you called me back here to help you and I missed out on the last two weeks." That was his excuse. It was all my fault that he was drinking again.

Faye was born in winter 2014 and Bob performed the usual fatherly birth-duties, I was happy that he was there but was not feeling safe and secure. I could smell alcohol on his breath and knew that he would be alone with our two toddlers until I could make it home to protect them. I couldn't rest while I was back on the ward, Faye was beautiful, and I spent hours in thankful silence that she was healthy and didn't require any additional care, but I couldn't take my mind of Louise and Patrick's vulnerability with Bob. I requested to be discharged early from hospital and given this was my third c-section, and well adapted to the pain, they allowed me to go home within forty-eight hours.

The next six weeks, I patiently recovered. Within the first week, I was grocery shopping with the three kids because Bob was back to his routine of early departure, with late and drunk arrivals at home. He would occasionally prepare dinner, and I quietly waited for him to prove to me that things had changed. They didn't. And after six weeks, I advised him of the vow I made to myself to allow him my 6 week 'recovery' time to prove that he was still the man I married, even if it was in a reduced capacity. He bowed his head. He knew he had let us all down. We separated at that time and he moved out immediately.

Life began to find a new rhythm, my Al Anon meetings continued, and I was able to distance myself from his accusations and his request for money. I still had faith that my husband would come back to me one day. Our custody mediation sessions were peaceful, he admitted his self-control issues and willingly agreed to breath testing before visits with the kids. The man I loved was still in there somewhere, it was up to him now, to find himself and I was all for his recovery.

The next few months were our hardest. He had stumbled into a relationship with a woman he had met in rehab.

His new girlfriend, Sarah*, was a drug addict, she was controlling and vicious. She answered my texts on his phone, pretending to be him. She referred to our kids as her 'spiritual children' and had threatened to 'wait until they're older and tell them all about the things I'd done to their father.' She dictated the rules of Bob and my relationship. We weren't allowed to speak to each other unless she was there; Bob wasn't allowed to visit the kids without her; and when he called me to talk to the kids, I was not allowed to speak. This last 'rule' was a fun one. Our children were too young to understand telephone protocol, so "Hello," and nods of the head is all they received. I was then, of course, admonished because I didn't assist with the phone call.

There was no situation where I could do the right thing. The emotional control that Sarah had over me, caused me to have panic attacks, and I vividly remember the night of the 30th June 2015 when I received a phone call from Bob.

On the night in question, Sarah and Bob had been together for three months. I had returned home from work and I had the three children in the bathtub. I answered my phone tentatively, fearing the wrath I would receive for speaking to Bob myself instead of giving the phone to the wet kids.

It was Sarah.

The conversation didn't go as I expected, she didn't yell at me for answering the phone. My fear was not realised, but my relief was short-lived.

Sarah told me that Bob had suffered a heart attack and she wasn't sure if he was alive. She confirmed that the ambulance was there, and I told her I'd be at their unit soon. I called my mum, and she came to look after the kids.

I arrived at their unit, and the front door was open. Sarah was so unhinged, I considered that her call was a hoax and I expected her to be waiting inside the door with a weapon, ready to kill me. I hesitantly approached the unit, with the intention that if I heard voices or laughter, I'd leave quietly and go home.

I reached their front door; the unit was thick with cigarette smoke. I found Sarah in their bedroom. I could see Bob's feet, then his legs, he had long pyjama pants on and his chest was bare. His hands were twisted into seizure-like balls. He was dead.

Sarah had rushed to me as I fell into her arms. I cried out in anguish; all hate was gone from me in that moment. We were just two distraught women who had just lost the man they loved. I don't know how long I stood there, comforted in an embrace by the evil person who had made my life hell.

Thousands of thoughts were competing for attention but one stood out, above all the others. *I wasn't there when he needed me.* I released myself from her and kneeled beside the bed, Bob's arms were stretched out towards me. I touched his hand. It was ice cold and stiff. He'd been dead for a long time. I stood up so suddenly that tripped backwards.

I accused Sarah of killing him and bumped into an ambulance officer as I left the unit. When I asked how long Bob had been dead, he quoted, 'Hours and hours.' I ran to my car and called the police. 'Bob' had been texting me from his phone only 20 minutes earlier to arrange a time to drop off the kids in the morning. Sarah had to have known that Bob was dead when she was texting me from his phone.

After months of waiting for results, the coroner finally identified that Bob had died from dilated cardiomyopathy, exacerbated by a mixed drug toxicity – all prescribed, but taken with his familiar disregard for caution. A natural death caused by his own poor life choices.

When I questioned her 'story' and why she was messaging me from his phone, and why she didn't call the ambulance sooner, I was told by the coroner, that 'people do strange things when they are grieving', and he dismissed her as unwell. I had to agree on both counts.

While organising Bob's funeral, I ensured that Sarah chose a song and allowed her to have a moment to share her thoughts of Bob and provide her space to grieve. I was called, 'gracious' for giving her this opportunity. In reality, I was terrified of what she would do to me if I didn't.

Sarah turned up to Bob's funeral, drunk. Her obituary claimed he had recently embraced Christianity; however, anyone who knew him could attest to his strict Roman Catholic upbringing and abhorrence of any faith. She explained in detail to the funeral attendees about her previous rapes and abuse, and how Bob saved her from this. She began to talk about me and how awful I was as a person and how much of a bad person I was. I decided my children didn't need to hear what she was saying and walked out with them. The rest of the guests followed me. She was asked to return to her seat by the funeral director, and when she refused, was escorted to her seat. As we all began to return to the chapel, she stood up and screamed, 'She did it!

She killed her husband!' While pointing at me with my children. She was then escorted out of the chapel, yelling and screaming.

Bob didn't have a will, so his estate was split between me, the kids, and Sarah. She was identified as his 'dependent' because they were residing together. It was a frustrating decision, but I knew that once she had the money, she would leave me alone.

Once all the official duties of a widowed wife were over, I returned to my routines with our children. Life was peaceful, but my mind was restless. I fought with my grief for a long time.

On one hand, I was so relieved that my children would not be co-parented by an alcoholic father and his erratic and manipulative girlfriend. The fear that Sarah would turn my children against me as they aged was now gone. The fear I had that she was going to be a mother to my children (they were apparently engaged to be married), was gone. I was happy to be raising my children alone, we had peaceful but fulfilling routines that were not marred by hostility, confusion or control. I was also relieved for Bob, that he was now at rest. His last few years seemed haunted with a demon that he couldn't find a way to control, and it drained the light that he once had for life.

On the other hand, I was utterly distraught. My beautiful, enigmatic, life loving, 'Bob O'clock' was gone, and along with it, all hope that my children would get to experience his infectious passion and enthusiasm for life, love, people and bikes. He left a gaping hole in the world of anyone who had the pleasure of meeting him, and the Earth has never really spun in quite the same way without him in it.

I learned that year, that grief doesn't have a path, there is no 'normal' way to fall apart, however, every single emotion that you feel when your love no longer has a place to go, is totally normal.

You're allowed to feel more than one emotion at one time, even if the emotions are relief that they are gone and total devastation that they're never coming back. I've learned that there's even a name for this, we call it 'bittersweet'.

I've remarried now, and my new husband has embraced my grief. We always pay tribute to Bob when 8.08 appears in our lives, and, along with his friends and family who live in all parts of the world, we celebrate with a drink at 8.08 on Bob's special days every year.

Bob O'clock will always be a time dedicated to the life of a man who threw so much love at everyone he met, who always had energy to share, but who found his end too soon.

Alice Monaghan *lives in Queensland with her husband and their blended family of five kids. Driven by curiosity and a deep love of learning, her free time is filled with an endless rotation of hobbies. A witty introvert with a love for a good story, Alice enjoys sharing her unique personal experiences with anyone who has the time to listen. This is her first time seeing her words in print.*

Memoir of a Morning: What I Wish I'd Known - a Retrospective

JJ Collins

To laugh often and much; to win the respect of intelligent people and the affection of children; to earn the appreciation of honest critics and endure the betrayal of false friends; to appreciate the beauty; to find the best in others; to leave the world a bit better, whether by a healthy child, a garden patch or a redeemed social condition; to know even one life has breathed easier because you have lived. This is to have succeeded!" (Ralph Waldo Emerson)[1]

A Cold July Dusk

The alarm goes off at 4:45 am.

Uggh. I don't have to get up; not really. But I should. I didn't go at all last week due to the bad weather. Who the hell goes swimming – outdoors – in July?

Take thy beak from out my heart and take thy form from off my door.[2]

The idea of getting out of bed feels like an eyrie raven watching over me. Nevermore – hah! I twist and my back cracks – just a bit, but in three places. See, no need to go anywhere. Your back's fine.

'It's only the beginning of winter, though. The cold is just going to get worse. You might as well make the most of it now,' I say, trying to convince myself to take the advice I'd so willingly hand out to someone else while standing in the doorway with my sherpa dressing gown on and no intention of leaving the house.

I glance at my phone as the snooze alarm goes off for the third time. Fine! After turning the alarm off, I dare to look at my weather app. I check the temperature outside, knowing that it's probably going to be counterintuitive.

It's nine degrees! Well, that's not so bad, I think, until ... 'feels like' 4.5.

Ahh, fuck!

Alright, you're awake now. Get up! Just get up. Just. Get. Up.

I wish I'd known how beautiful, peaceful, invigorating and motivating the cold dusk air can be at this time of the morning. Maybe I'd be used to it by now.

At 5:20 am, I'm finally in the car after tripping over a pillow, getting probably a little too snappy with the husbo (after I was the one who woke him up), cleaning up cat shit from the bathroom floor (while thanking the lord that at least the cat had the good sense to go on the tiles), chucking the pooped-on mats in the washing machine, pacing the kitchen and finally deciding not to have breakfast or coffee because if I sit still now, I'll end up right back asleep. Great start! Never mind, you can worry about that later. Sort out the rest of your crap when you get back. Who the hell is going to know about all the stuff you haven't done before you left the house? Grab your shit! Let's just go!

Chin up, tits out, onward!

I wish I'd known that perfectionism is not a prerequisite for self-care.

Driving to the leisure centre takes less than ten minutes but I'm way behind on my normal reading schedule so I turn on my audiobook and reverse out with my windows still fogged up. So dumb! I can't see anything, and I can't focus on the book either. Wipers, shift into drive and rewind.

I arrive. The girls behind the desk are always chatty this time of the morning – probably because they're not the crazy people about to go swimming in 'feels like' 4.5 degrees. Can you see me rolling my eyes? They have heaters and jumpers, and we chat for a moment about the three people who still turned up to do their swim on the day of the storm last week. I admire the willpower of my fellow lunatics.

I wish I'd known much sooner that I did not need permission to start taking care of myself without that kind of willpower. Imagine how great I'd feel.

The steam rising from the water against the dark, inky-blue sky is utterly mesmerising. I've tried to snap a few pics, but I can never seem to capture the way it makes me feel. That reminds me, I must have a play around with the camera settings on this phone. It can't be that hard. I'm vaguely intelligent, right? Right?

Sitting here, it's a cosy feeling – despite the fact that I'm still quite cold, even with my Ugg boots, trackies and fleecy hoodie over my swimmers. I could just sit here on the stairs and watch the steam for the longest time, staring out at the stars, being reminded of the absolute insignificance of all of us. And there are no ducks today. That's a shame. Maybe I haven't completely shaken the raven just yet on this frosty morning.

I wish I'd known to stop and take in these precious moments every ... single ... time they present themselves. Maybe I would have had more of an appreciation for the smaller things.

As I step down the stairs, lowering myself into the water while adjusting my goggles, I'm reminded of the whiteboard I saw when I entered the leisure centre foyer. It said that the Program Pool (the 25 m pool that I swim in because it's warmer – even though this means I have to do twice as many laps) was 29.2 degrees. Not sure what the 'feels like' temperature is but it sure as hell isn't 29.2! Jeebus!

As a result of this seemingly completely mental practice, I've learned that my body does in fact heat up quite a bit once I get moving. It's just the getting moving part that's difficult, although I need the pep talk less and less now, so there's a little win.

They stack up, don't they? The little wins. All of a sudden, you're doing something that makes you feel amazing on so many levels. Something that everyone you tell envies you for. Count them – those little wins – because they do matter more than they seem.

I wish I'd known to focus on the little wins, not just the lack of big ones.

A kilometre is the distance. Four times a week is the goal. But, in July and August, the goal is just to go. She says this with a sheepish blush on her face, knowing it sounds stupendously easy, while it is, in fact, becoming increasingly difficult as the weather becomes colder and colder. Just turn up as often as you can and do the kilometre. You're doing so much better than the same woman six months ago who didn't do this at all. Have a bit of faith in yourself.

If there's one thing I've learned about myself, it's that I can talk myself out of doing anything. Oh, my wordy lordy yes, Janelle[3] – especially when it means that putting my own needs aside will make someone else feel better; particularly the male kind of person (not the husbo though, he's tops). But that's what we're taught aren't we? That to be a good woman means meeting everyone else's needs at the expense of your own. That putting yourself first is selfish.

I wish I'd known that having a little more faith in myself did not, in fact, mean I was conceited. After all, you can't give what you haven't got.

And So, It Begins

I warm up on my first lap with slow peaceful breaststroke, making sure to pull my shoulder blades far enough back that they touch each time as I come up for air. This is the spot. The part of my spine that still gives me grief, even all these years after that injury. The place I can rarely stretch out enough to bring any kind of relief. It feels amazing.

This is how I spend the first three to five laps each morning – stretching and strengthening that tight spot. Slowly though. Not too fast. There's plenty more to be seen and admired to calm and gently awaken the mind. It's still dark outside – probably only 5:40 am or thereabouts – and the reflections of the water's movement on the tiled floor of the heated pool are breathtaking, lit only by a few small artificial lights and a floodlight at the top of the nearby hill. They shimmer and sparkle in a multitude of depths, floating around with seemingly no real direction, reminiscent of the fairies in gossamer dresses in the stories I used to read to my daughter twenty-ish years ago, before she towered over me. She was so, so innocent.

I wish I'd known just how fast that time with tiny her would fly by. I would have slowed ... right ... down.

Under the water; how fabulous! Warm, beautiful and quiet. This has definitely become my happy place. The only thing I can hear is the gentle hum of the pump a few metres away, until I slowly come up for air, arching my back, wishing I were a mermaid or some sort of gilled creature, any kind, so I could spend all my days here.

The kids in the swimming club – big kids, teenagers – are pushing themselves in the freezing cold, trying to beat their best times, Trying to get fit. Trying to become *achievers*. The ones up on the seats waiting their turn chatter and giggle and muck around. How special is that kind of comradery? That's rhetorical. It's so special. I hope they succeed and that their time at swim club – at 5:30 am – builds some of the most precious friendships they can treasure for a lifetime.

People come and people go. Some of them I miss, but the best ones have put up with me for a bit and that I treasure.

I wish I'd known how to be a better friend. But, then again, things might be different.

A Reflection of My Own

Although, on the days when I'm feeling overwhelmed, this time is for nothing but exercise and meditation – counting only strokes of the arms and laps of the pool and taking in the admiration of the simplistic beauty of the bubbles with every exhale – today was one of reflection. It's not really in my control. What comes just seems to come. I find reflection an important tool for self-evaluation but it's really easy to wish your life away, get caught up in the 'what-if' moments. It's a perfect breeding ground for anxiety, which can, and will, eat you alive if you're not paying attention. I remind myself not to stay in the past for too long.

I wish I'd known how much damage spending too much time in the past could do. I would have saved myself a lot of angst.

You know how childhood stories are all about warnings and lessons that are full of metaphors? Why is it that we don't really pay attention to those until we are older? I think a part of the answer may lie somewhere in the fact that it's not until we start to *unlearn* what we've been taught as children that we give ourselves permission to question what we've been told. We allow ourselves to dig a little deeper into those 'silly' children's stories and, consequently, see the 'hidden' truths that present themselves to us in myriad different ways, based on our own experiences and perceptions as we get older.

I wish I'd known that I didn't have to have it all figured out because my mind and my views would change so much anyway – and that's more than okay. It's actually quite normal.

Take the yellow brick road, for example. A long, winding road fraught with danger, twists and turns, bumps and evil enemies who are trying to trick you because they're so invested in their own agendas. Poppies, poppies, poppies will put them to sleep.[4] The point is that it's about the journey. It's about keeping your eye on the prize. Everything you ever needed, you already have. Despite the trials and tribulations, you'll end up exactly where you're supposed to be anyway.

Trust the process.

How about the talking flowers in *Alice in Wonderland*? She's nothing but a wheeed![5] But Alice stands up for herself. She holds true to herself, despite the judgement and criticisms. She comes out of it a little wet but that will dry off, no sweat. These are the reminders. They are the memory cues I need while tumble-turning in a pool in the cold dark of the morning, wondering why things aren't working out the way society tells me they should. Do you think it could be my higher self trying to communicate with my inner child? That's rhetorical too. Of course it is.

I wish I'd known to pay more attention to my higher self and my inner child years ago. They're wiser than I gave them credit for.

Left arm goes over and touches my leg as my right arm comes over. I take a big, deep inhale. It's lap ten. My face is straight down, looking directly at the small, white, square tiles on the bottom of the pool. A slow exhale and the bubbles rush along my cheeks and neck as they rise to the surface like liberated little soldiers that have been working to keep me going. You're free now, little dudes. Free!

This next big inhale reminds me of the value of breath. It reminds me of the value of those big, deep, full breaths that stretch and enlarge your stomach and your diaphragm. I've lived a life filled with stress, trauma and pain, mostly due to injuries. When that catalyst hits, breathing can become very shallow. Not like an anxiety attack, these ones creep up. Sometimes I don't even realise I'm doing it until I find myself dealing with the repercussions.

This morning, in the midst of those big deep breaths, looking at the tall palm tree swaying in the wind and lit up by the floodlight beside it, I'm reminded of how valuable they are and how healing meditative breathing can be. I add that to my mental to-do list as the next arm goes over and the scenery changes to a yellow pumphouse under the stars on the other side of the pool.

I wish I spent more time on meditation; I might be calmer.

As I ponder where I am and what I'm doing and how, I've come to realise that water truly is the elixir of life. Over the last six months, I've tripled my daily water consumption and undertaken what, for me, is a life-altering practice. Stretching and strengthening my spine, my hips, shoulders, neck and jaw with no pressure on my joints and plenty of resistance from the water. It seems so simple. It's like the answer was right there in front of me this whole time. Right there in plain sight.

I truly wish I knew just how much good plain old water was going to do me. There's no need to overcomplicate anything, really. Much less taking care of yourself.

It's lap fifteen now – I count up and back as one lap, doing twenty in total. If you're counting along, don't judge me. I need to trick myself. Hey, whatever works, right? I've noticed that, as I tire a little, I'm no longer swimming in a straight line.

Oh, my God!

Whatever! No-one shares my lane at this time of the morning anyway.

This brings my attention to alignment – particularly alignment in love. I could've saved myself so much pain – so ... much ... pain – had I known that being understood was next-level intimacy.

No. No, that's not true. I did know that. My thoughts and feelings just didn't match my actions. I closed all the doors out of fear and then said I couldn't find it. Sometimes, it's difficult to admit how different things would've been if I didn't try to justify the red flag away. Didn't try to make excuses for the bad behaviour of others. Wasn't so out of alignment with *myself* that I believed everyone else must know better than me because I was missing something in my own life. Pretty sad, huh?

Do you think anyone would notice if I shed a tiny tear into my goggles for my younger self? Pretty funny, though – I reckon – all foggy and shit. I think I've heard a song about realigning. I'll have to look that up.

I wish I'd know that I'd be okay if I walked away and didn't try to fix the red flag bearer. But then again, who and where would I be right now had I not had those experiences?

I think a move back to breaststroke is in order. Back to the slower breathing. Maybe some music will help. Also, whoever said that heavy metal music is no good for mental health is just plain wrong! There was some other band going on about it not being noise pollution or something, wasn't there? I think I'd literally go insane if my favourite bands didn't keep smashing out tunes about shit that's hard, so we can all feel that sense of unity and togetherness. The echo of the inner chaos of humanity. Plus, how good is live music, honestly? I wish I'd gone to more live shows.

More specifically, I wish I'd known to prioritise that feeling you get in a crowd of like-minded sweaty onlookers who are screaming their hearts out and jumping around to their favourite songs – the ones that make your heart feel like it's on fire. I wish I'd known that the adrenaline, the volume, and the buzz of the swarm is actually extremely healing.

Home to the Kitties

Getting out of the pool is sometimes harder than getting in. But there's a silver lining here too. Last year, some kid rear-ended my car and wrote it off. Yes, that was crappy and so was the leg injury. Blah, blah – let's not dwell on that – but this meant I got new car. It also meant I can now turn the ignition on from an app and preheat the car on cold July mornings at dusk.

Winning!

Anyway, I digress. After drying off, I rush out to my toasty car and chuck the audiobook back on. It's pretty disappointing but I think

I've guessed the outcome of this character. I hope I'm wrong. I'd really prefer a shocking twist.

When I get home, my gorgeous kitty cat is waiting on the porch for me as usual. He jumps on top of the letterbox, luring me over with his chirpy trills and meows. We have a cuddle and a scratch as the pinks and purples of sunrise begin to arrive. He follows me inside and hides under the desk my treasured friend hand-painted for me. He's ready to play peek-a-boo as he so often does. (This is not the same cat who shit on the bathroom floor earlier, either.)

This cat is one-in-a-million, I swear, but today he's looking up the stairs, wondering who's in that bathroom up there. With his big hazel eyes and long shadowy whiskers, he's making all sorts of sweet little kitty cat sounds, and I wonder if I'm actually going insane, or if the spirit of our little boy is actually in that cat.

I wish I'd known just what grief can do. I might have gone a little easier on myself and those around me.

***

Acknowledgments to a very small few – of the people who keep me sane with their brilliant works.

1. *What is Success?* by Ralph Waldo Emerson
2. *The Raven* by Edgar Allan Poe
3. Chenille, by Magda Szubanski, *Full Frontal*
4. *The Wizard of Oz* by Frank L. Baum
5. *Alice in Wonderland* by Lewis Carroll

JJ Collins is a forty-something-year-old woman living in Sydney with her much-loved husband and two kitty cats. She has one gorgeous grown-up girl and grew up down the coast a bit. JJ loves all things artsy and crafty, and this little chapter is her first official writing endeavour. So, welcome to the official 'dipping of the toe into the water'.

Breaking the Silence

Jo Jo Sparkle

I met him in 2014.

It started like so many love stories do, with hope. A mutual friend introduced us and there was an immediate connection. We laughed easily, shared stories and bonded quickly. I was a single mother to a beautiful three-and-a-half-year-old daughter, and he was kind to her, gentle even. In those first few months, he seemed thoughtful and considerate. After so long on my own, it felt like a blessing – like someone who truly cared had finally come into our lives.

By mid-2014, I'd made a big decision. I moved closer to him, hoping to build a life together. I left behind my comfort zone, my familiar surroundings and my own sense of safety in the name of love and the promise of family. In hindsight, I realise that moment marked the beginning of a long and painful chapter of my life ... one that would nearly break me.

The first six months were a whirlwind. We were in love, or so I thought. We spent time with friends and family, talked about the future and I fell pregnant in August. We were overjoyed – or at least I was. But joy quickly turned to grief when we lost our baby girl in October. The pain of that loss was immense.

Even during those early months, there were red flags. Small, uneasy moments that I pushed aside. I knew he had, as he put it, a 'bit of a sordid past'. I didn't ask questions. I believed in second chances. I believed people could change. More than anything, I wanted our relationship to work.

In December 2014, I fell pregnant again, and that's when the truth came out. He sat me down, his face tight with tension – but a sly smirk – and confessed something that shattered the fragile world we were building. He had taken a life in the past.

I was stunned. I couldn't comprehend what I was hearing. I felt betrayed. I was terrified and unsure of what to do next. But I was pregnant and a part of me still wanted to believe he could be the man I hoped for.

From that moment, everything changed. He started using money as a weapon, refusing to contribute, hiding it or using it as leverage. The kindness he once showed my daughter faded first into cold indifference, and then outright cruelty. He became increasingly aggressive and abusive, verbally and emotionally. The lies multiplied. The mask he'd worn so well in the beginning began to slip.

My pregnancy was difficult. I suffered from hyperemesis gravidarum, an extreme form of morning sickness that left me hospitalised multiple times. I was physically weak and emotionally exhausted, trying to protect a child growing inside me while shielding my daughter from his rage.

As the pregnancy progressed, his aggression escalated. He'd scream, belittle me and lash out with terrifying intensity. My daughter became a target too. Her spirit dimmed under the weight of his anger and I felt powerless to stop it.

At thirty-one weeks, the baby tried to come early. It felt like even my body was rejecting the chaos around me. I held on until thirty-eight weeks and finally went into labour.

Instead of being a moment of joy, it was another chapter of fear. I felt intimidated and alone in the delivery room. I didn't know how to ask that he not be there. His presence loomed like a dark cloud. A moment that should've been beautiful felt shadowed by dread.

After the birth, I hoped things would get better.

They didn't.

He showed no interest in our newborn son. He wouldn't help, wouldn't provide, wouldn't even pretend to be present. Instead, he disappeared – off to the pub, chasing cash, chasing freedom and then blaming me when the baby was sleeping. I was left alone with two children, trying to survive, to heal and to understand how everything had gone so wrong.

Then came the moment I'll never forget.

In a rage, he locked my daughter in the car in forty-one-degree heat, then stood beside it listening to her beg him to let her out. He stood beside the car with the baby, because to him that child was HIS son and she didn't matter anymore. I was in the supermarket getting cold drinks, and when I came out and heard her pleas, I realised that he'd nearly taken her life.

Writing those words still sends shivers through my body. The terror of that day still lives with me. It was a breaking point. A moment of clarity. I knew then that if I didn't act, we might not survive.

In April 2015, I finally found the strength to call the police. They came with weapons drawn, storming into our home to ensure we were safe. I remember holding my children close, shaking, trying to believe that maybe … just maybe … this was the beginning of our freedom.

I filed for a no-contact protection order.

The next few weeks were a blur of police interviews, paperwork, legal advice and court appearances. I found myself having to explain, over and over, what had happened. I had to revisit the abuse in detail. Relive moments I was trying to forget. I told my story in statements, timelines and affidavits. Each time I told it, it hurt a little more. Yet, with each telling, I also reclaimed a piece of power I'd lost.

Getting the protection order was both empowering and terrifying. It meant that, legally, couldn't come near us. But it also meant the threat had been made visible. I knew him. I knew how he could twist and manipulate. I knew how he saw consequences not as warnings but as challenges. So I packed what I could in the middle of the night and I moved out.

I hoped we were free but the nightmare didn't end there. He followed us. He found our new address, harassed my parents and lurked in the shadows of our new life. When he followed us, when he harassed my parents, it confirmed my fear – paper alone wouldn't protect us. I was constantly looking over my shoulder, afraid to let my guard down.

We packed up, quietly and quickly, and left. We moved to a new place, further away this time. No-one knew where we went, not even most of our friends. We just vanished, like ghosts, starting again from nothing. A new town. A fresh start. My daughter was five-and-a-half. My son, just seven months old. We were broken but we were safe, and that's where the healing began.

Our new home wasn't perfect, but it was quiet. For the first time in a long time, I could sleep without fear of what might happen in the middle of the night. My children began to smile more. My daughter, who'd once been outgoing and bubbly, slowly began to trust the world again. My baby boy, too young to understand everything, could grow without the constant cloud of violence overhead.

But, peace didn't come all at once. It wasn't a straight path. It never is. The trauma lingered like a shadow, always behind us. My body was still in survival mode. I'd jump at sudden noises, flinch at raised voices and carried constant tension in my shoulders. Even though he was physically no longer in our lives, he was still there – in our minds, in our behaviours and in the fear that clung to us like fog.

I remember one night vividly. My daughter woke up screaming from a nightmare. She was shaking, crying out his name and begging him to stop. She was only six but her dreams carried the weight of memories no child should bear. I held her, rocked her, whispered that we were safe now. That he couldn't hurt us anymore. But even as I said the words, I wasn't sure I believed them myself.

PTSD became part of our everyday lives. It looks different for each of us. For me, it's the panic attacks that come out of nowhere. For my daughter, it's the way she shuts down when someone raises their voice. For my son, it's the way he clings to me like his life depends on it because, for so long, it had.

I didn't have all the answers. I was learning how to mother two traumatised children while healing from my own wounds. I often felt like I was failing, like I wasn't doing enough. But every day we got up and we kept going. We'd survived the worst. Now we just had to figure out how to live. Over time, I found bits of myself again.

I started by reaching out for help. This was something I'd once seen as a weakness but I'd come to understand it was an act of strength. I connected with local women's services and domestic violence services. I attended therapy. I joined support groups. Talking to other women who'd been through similar horrors reminded me I wasn't alone. It helped me put words to what I'd endured. It helped me let go of the guilt, the shame and the self-blame that had rooted itself deep in my heart.

I watched my daughter begin to thrive. She made friends. She started to laugh again – real, belly-deep laughs that reminded me of who she was before the violence. My son hit his milestones. He grew strong and curious. He loves animals and cars and has the kindest little soul. In them, I saw light return to our lives.

But healing isn't linear. There were days I wanted to give up. Days where the flashbacks were too strong, where I questioned whether leaving had really changed anything. The system wasn't always kind. There were moments when I felt like I had to prove I was a victim, as if my word alone wasn't enough. The emotional toll of the court proceedings, of facing him again, even across a courtroom, was soul crushing. But I kept going. For my kids. For myself.

I started journalling. Writing became a form of therapy. I wrote letters I never sent. I wrote down every feeling, every fear and every moment I wanted to forget. Slowly, I began to understand that survival was more than just getting through each day; it was reclaiming my story. I didn't want to be defined by what he did to us. I wanted to be defined by what we did next.

We created new traditions: birthday parties filled with laughter; movie nights snuggled under blankets; dance parties in the living room just because we could. I let the kids decorate their rooms however they wanted. We planted flowers in the yard. We made our house a home – a sanctuary.

Years passed. The nightmares became less frequent. The fear softened; though it never disappeared entirely. I became more open about our story – not to dwell on the pain but to show others that it's possible to come out the other side. That no matter how broken you feel, you can rebuild. You can rise.

Now, nine years later, we're still healing. Trauma doesn't vanish; it becomes a part of who you are. But we're not broken anymore. We're stitched together with strength and love. My daughter is a teenager now. She's fierce and wise beyond her years. She knows the value of her voice and she uses it. My son is in school, full of energy and light. He has no memory of the man who hurt us but I've taught him about kindness, empathy and respect. He knows what love is supposed to feel like.

And me?

I'm no longer the woman who doubted her worth. I'm not the woman who stayed silent. I'm the woman who survived. The mother who protected her children. The voice that refused to be silenced.

We still have hard days. PTSD doesn't go away because time passes. But now, we have tools. We have support. We have each other. There are moments when I catch a glimpse of who I used to be before him. I see her in the mirror sometimes. She's stronger now but she still cries when the memories come. And that's okay. Crying isn't weakness; it's proof that I still feel. That I still care. That I'm still healing. This chapter of our lives, this story of survival, isn't just about pain – it's about resilience. It's about hope. It's about the truth that, even in the darkest times, there is light. And sometimes, that light comes from within.

We are survivors.

We are still here.

And we will never go back.

This story is not just about what we endured; it's about what we became. We're not victims lost in the past; we're survivors rising into our future. We carry our scars, not with shame but with pride. Each one tells a story of strength, of love, of a mother who refused to give up and of children who refused to be broken. Our journey isn't over, but every step forward is proof that healing is possible.

If you're reading this, if you're in the dark, unsure and afraid, know this – there is life after fear.

There is light after darkness.

You, too, are stronger than you know.

Jo Jo Sparkle *is a first-time author with a powerful story of resilience, strength and survival. She shares her raw and honest story of overcoming domestic violence and building a new life filled with hope and healing. Through her writing, Jo Jo aims to give voice to others who have faced similar struggles and to remind them that growth is possible, even after the darkest of times. When she's not writing, Jo Jo enjoys spending time with her children, taking them on holidays, cooking, and creating new memories. This is her debut published work.*

Abused to Ablaze

Twee Shaw

I should be dead.

I've survived literal and metaphorical fires: abuse, grief, chronic illness, crashes, loss and trauma – the kind of flames that consume most people whole. But, instead of destroying me, those fires forged me. They burned away the lies, the masks and the self-abandonment. What came out of the flames wasn't a victim – it was a blaze!

My name is Twee Shaw, and I am now SURE about who I am, my mission and the women I serve. This is my story of going from abused to ablaze, and the birth of The FIRE Revolution.

Lava or Leave It!

I've always been described as being 'extreme' and 'extra'. They haven't been wrong. I was either 'lava' – coming in hot, fiery and all-in – or I was the complete opposite: procrastinating, avoiding, numb and 'leave it' or avoid at all costs.

As the eldest child, I was either on top of the mountain planting my victory flag or washed out and drowning. There was really never any middle ground. Much like my attention deficit hyperactivity disorder (ADHD) and neurodiversity that had me bouncing between overdrive and burnout, I either burned bright or burned out. When you live like that long enough, you start to believe that's all you are: either too much or nothing at all.

To make things even spicier, I came from a family of maths geniuses, maths teachers, engineers and chess champions. My son Maximus inherited it too. But me? I had to have dyscalculia – numbers dyslexia. Numbers terrorised me the way Brussels sprouts or spiders might freak others out. Calculations and memorising phone numbers was impossible without a calculator. I was the one with zero coordination and a fear of numbers. I was the one who didn't fit into the mould. I was the odd one out – the failure.

I told myself I was broken because I couldn't 'get it' like the rest of them. What I didn't know then was that lava doesn't follow formulas. Fire is unpredictable with lots of variables that don't always care for neat equations. Fire creates its own path.

Reclaiming My Name

Even my name was used against me.

In the British dictionary, 'twee' is defined as dainty, delicate, cutesy – the opposite of fierce and strong. For years, I believed it and twisted myself into that definition. I tried to be small enough, sweet enough and soft enough, all in an attempt to minimise attention and to survive. But I was never meant to be 'twee' in this sense of the word.

My Vietnamese name means 'over vast waters into the horizon'. That meaning carried both beauty and irony because water became my fear. Despite living on an island state surrounded by water, I never learned to swim. I had multiple near-death experiences in water and the waves seemed to remind me of how small, powerless and unanchored I felt in life.

But when I chose to reclaim my truth, I was able to say my name, Twee Shaw, with confidence and power because I'm unapologetically on FIRE – fearless, independent, resilient, empowered.

But I didn't always feel this way.

Refugee Roots

My mother and I escaped Vietnam and were nearly a month lost at sea before we arrived at 'Pula Bidong' Island refugee camp in Malaysia. Known as 'Hell Isle', it was a space the size of a football field, but once the most populated place on Earth. We'd been deceived by a man who claimed to be a captain but carried no map or compass.

That pattern of wanting to believe the best in people, not rocking the boat, and staying quiet to survive nearly cost us our lives. We drifted dangerously, at risk of capture, starvation, pirates and worse. Food was regularly taken from me, and survival meant silence and endurance.

From there, we were sponsored and brought to the 'apple isle' of Tasmania. It was here I first learned to become hyper-independent – unable to trust others to do what they said they would. I carried the belief that if I didn't do it myself, it wouldn't be done, and that lesson became both my survival and my burden. In that new world, my mother and I faced racism, and I grew up feeling singled out. Too fast, too fiery, too ambitious – too much of everything! For years, I tried to shrink into less.

Geology as Destiny

I studied geology at the University of Tasmania, never realising it would become the perfect metaphor for my life because what is geology if not pressure and heat transforming raw matter into diamonds, into volcanoes and into entire landscapes?

My life has been one long geological event with plenty of extreme tectonic shifts and movements: child abuse, sexual abuse, grief, domestic violence, fire after fire, crashes, falls, pressure, and heat – again and again – all reshaping me into something unrecognisable, even to myself. Yet, in that furnace I became forged like metamorphic rock and transformed by intense heat and pressure. I was reshaped, reformed and no longer what I once was. Just like joints in the landscape, old lines of weakness from deep time would suddenly reappear at the surface. Old wounds, old fractures, patterns from the past showing up again in the present and demanding to be acknowledged before the landscape – or my life – could stabilise.

Before leaving Tasmania, it felt like a volcanic eruption of passion and purpose. I was working with traumatised refugee youth and witnessed incredible transformations – my very first hot lava experience. In helping them achieve their own breakthroughs, I was experiencing my own healing too. I shared their stores at Refugee Week events, carrying their courage as part of my own. That season of fire and growth culminated in me winning the Tasmanian Young Achiever's Award for the work I did. It set me up for a move to Sydney, carrying momentum and confidence into my next big challenge.

When I moved to Sydney, my internal fire was sparked and I rode the high of the tsunami wave of success. I experienced the highs of love, adventure, business success, material collections and comforts.

But the bigger the rise, the harder the fall.

Divorce stripped me of everything – homes, businesses, stability and love. It left me with debt, legal fees, betrayal, guilt and shame. I told myself it was punishment for not being enough. That breaking my wedding vows sworn before the archbishop meant I deserved to suffer. When my next relationship also failed, I ignored the legal advice to pursue financial settlement or child support. I convinced myself that I was honouring my son's desire to have no connection to his father – but the truth was so much darker. Deep down, I believed that money should be earned honestly and given freely. To accept something I had to fight for would come with bitter energy that would drown us in guilt and resentment. So, I chose struggle and convinced myself I was being noble and independent because it was more palatable than admitting I was depriving or robbing my own son thanks to my beliefs.

And then there was grief after the long goodbye.

Losing Dad – the only man who'd ever made me feel safe and who loved me without condition – was another fire. We watched a 120 kg, strong man and intellectual giant slowly and painfully forget who we were. Early-onset Alzheimer's forced us to watch this powerful force of nature slowly transform into a giant toddler – our very own non-verbal Benjamin Button – until the disease stole him from us completely. It was another stripping away. Another ash pile I was left sitting in with third-degree burns because it was a fire I didn't want to leave, knowing the darkness beyond it.

After losing Dad I fought harder for a relationship that was destroying me. I was scared I couldn't be the safety or strength for my son that Dad had been for me. By then, I was starting to believe that God was cruel and testing me. That I wasn't worthy of rewards or his love. That I should be allergic to joy and love in order to stay safe. Every time I'd built something I was proud of and loved, it was taken from me.

The Car Crash: Extra, Explosive and Unavoidable

I grew up around car accidents. Not the kind you watch on the news, but the kind you collect like a stamp set. By the time I was old enough to drive, I already had a backlog of crash stories, so when I finally got my licence, I avoided driving as much as possible. Not because I didn't want the freedom, but because I was terrified of what freedom in my hands could cost. I had this gnawing fear that I might cause an accident and I honestly didn't think I could live with the guilt of hurting someone.

And when I did drive? Let's just say I was creative with the rules. I used to keep my P plates on long after I had my full licence as a warning label for other drivers. My private joke was that the 'P' didn't stand for provisional; it stood for 'public service announcement' – please beware, I suck at this! Cue the classic 'bad Asian driver' stereotype. I was laughing about it before anyone else could. Humour became my shield and got me off the hook before anyone else could judge me. But underneath the jokes – the driving fear was real.

If there's one thing that's consistent about me it's that I don't do anything halfway. When I'm all in, I'm fully committed – even when it comes to accidents! Most people settle for a scrape to the bumper or swipe to their mirror but not me! The 'accident' I tried to avoid became a full-blown crash into a tree that set the car on fire. Black smoke billowed into the sky and could be seen far and wide. There was no hiding it. The crash exposed me for being extra once again. We were pulled out just before the car exploded. My world collapsed. I was unable to work and lost my sense of worth and purpose. I also lost my ability to dissociate and separate from my body, which had been my survival superpower.

The part that burned more than the flames was knowing that my blackout on the highway almost killed my child. That guilt hit harder than any collision. Heavier than the wreckage. And it wasn't just personal guilt, it was cultural. Generational. I'd grown up being taught that I was responsible for everyone's safety. Don't cause shame. Don't be a burden to your family. Yet here I was – broken, exposed, guilty. The volcano of shame erupted and there was no stuffing it back down.

At the hospital, I was separated from my child and forced to face the tsunami of reality – I was responsible for almost killing him and myself. The guilt of this truth was more horrific than my injuries or the state of the car. It clung to me like smoke I couldn't wash off. The worst part was that Maximus was adamant that my late dad had guided our car off the highway into the only tree that could stop us before we plunged into death.

I was angry with myself and wished I hadn't survived. My son may have sensed this because he developed his own anxiety about screaming at his mother to wake up as I was slumped unconscious over the wheel while accelerating towards my reckoning.

Strangely, after my licence was gone, I felt ... relief. No more pretending. No more hiding behind jokes. No more plastering on a smile while my stomach knotted with fear every time I touched the wheel.

Dissociation had always been my superpower and the way I survived abuse, trauma and silence. This time, however, I had no warning. I couldn't escape my body. I couldn't float away. Now, I thank God for that because the one thought that pierced my despair was if I'd left for eternity, my child would've been alone in that car. Abandoned. I could NOT let that be his last memory of me. So, I stayed.

The accident stopped me. Not just my car but my body, which I'd been racing through life – thrashed as if it were a formula one car – while ignoring every warning light, skipping every service and burning my body 'engine' to the ground. But here's the twist – the crash didn't break me; it actually forced me back into my body. Not gracefully. Not heroically. But truthfully.

The Aftermath

The crash stopped me cold. Not just physically in my car or with my body. It stopped my entire way of existing. I wish I could say, "That's when I stopped running." But the truth was I didn't stop. The Universe had to physically slam the brakes while God rejected my hope to see my dad again. Life forced me to face what I'd been outrunning. It was like a tectonic shift. The kind that rips landscapes apart and exposes the fault lines that have always been there. My crash was that earthquake, cracking open the ground beneath me and forcing me to finally confront the fractures I'd tried to bury over the years. Just like in geology, where ancient pressures suddenly rupture and reshape the land, the accident ruptured my carefully constructed survival strategies and exposed the deep fault lines of shame, fear and silence that had always run beneath my surface like bubbling magma, building in pressure.

A year later, standing with my clinical psychologist at the crash site and staring down at the burned-out shell of the car, I realised I was too. My son loves Kinder Surprise eggs for the mystery toy inside. Standing there, I felt like the Temu version: no joy, nothing inside. Worse yet, it was white chocolate – fake, empty and pretending to be chocolate. (Don't even start with me on white chocolate. There's no chocolate in it and I refuse to waste my calories or fire on something that pretends to be what it isn't.)

Anyway, that was the perfect description of me in that moment. A hollow, burned-out shell of a human. As we looked at the wreckage, all that remained of our car was a warped burned-out piece of bumper bar. Thin, useless armour that hadn't protected us. The wattle tree that had taken the full force of our impact and saved our lives was gone too. What stood between us and death no longer existed. There was no going back, no rewinding, no alternate ending. The only way now was through the fire. As my therapist stared in horror at what could have been, I felt only peace. No shock, no fear, just acceptance because I finally understood. Sometimes the fire doesn't just take – it clears. It strips away everything false so only the truth remains.

Every ache and injury became a painful reminder that I was alive. There was no more floating out of my body at the first hint of pain. My pain tethered me to reality like an anchor. Recovery was brutal and graphic – kind of like standing in front of a burned house of horrors, clearing debris before rebuilding. In that moment, it was clear I had to come home to myself before I could even think about building again.

The idea of coming home terrified me. I sought mentors like Peter Sage, Rory Kilmartin and Dr Joe Dispenza. I worked on healing my inner child while also trying to parent my actual child at the same time. Maximus, who'd watched me almost die, now carried his own trauma – terrified that one day I might not wake up. Every wince, every stumble reinforced his terror. Here was my precious boy, forced to parent me when, overcome with pain, I wet myself. He called ambulances and changed me before paramedics arrived. No child should carry the weight of that responsibility. The shame of it cut deeper than any physical pain, compounding the guilt of knowing I'd almost killed him. It filled my lungs and engulfed me in smoke I couldn't see beyond. The shame of that moment with my son was suffocating and near destroyed me while the familiar voices screamed louder: You're too broken to protect him – you'll never be a good mother. They reinforced my belief that Maximus deserved better than I was capable of.

Ironically, as devastating as it was, this too became part of the forge. The very thing I thought disqualified me – my brokenness – also became the fuel for my transformation. I was forced to confront what I'd been running from most of my life – my worth, my inner child, my fire. It was one of the darkest seasons of my life. There were nights I wished I hadn't made it out of that wreck, convinced my family would be better off without the burden of me. But the crash amplified what had always been there – the insatiable hunger that had never left me.

The Hunger

My former boss, Phil, once called it my 'starving child syndrome'. He used to call me a food monster with 'hollow legs' because, despite being mini snack-sized myself, I could out-eat most men at the table. It was funny on the surface but underneath it was the same scarcity wound – my insatiable hunger made visible. I was always hungry. I laughed it off and embraced it. But the truth was more raw – my hunger was never just about food; it was always about scarcity and lack and never feeling like I was enough.

With food I ate like I'd never see another meal. Deep down, my nervous system was wired to believe it might be my last. My gratitude for the meal was mixed with terror and fear that, were I were to waste any, the rice grains would turn to maggots and eat me alive.

With sex I craved intimacy, and I mistook attention for love. I sacrificed values, body, boundaries and pleasure for connection and to feel wanted.

With knowledge I consumed books and courses endlessly, hoarding them like precious jewels I was too afraid to wear because no matter how much I learned, it never felt like enough.

With money I was a sales gun and could make it easily but never kept it. To me, money represented abuse of power and excess. It felt dirty, dangerous, abusive and tainted – blood money. My parents were humanitarians, giving everything away, teaching me that good people sacrifice and share and bad people hoard and use it to control others. After my divorce, I wore my debt like punishment and atonement and carried the blind belief like scripture that it would bring nothing but pain and should not be enjoyed. I refused child support and convinced myself I was being independent and noble. In reality, I was depriving my son because I couldn't untangle my worth from my wounds.

No matter how much I consumed, it was never enough. Because the hunger wasn't just in my mind my body or my bank account. It was in my soul aching for me to come home.

It wasn't just about food, sex, knowledge or money. It was about the hunger for a childhood I never had. I was trying to reconnect with the child inside me, the girl who never got to be carefree or playful, who had to grow up too fast (while raising a child of my own) and trying to ignore the scared whisper: *you are not safe, you are not worthy, you will never be enough.*

How do you learn to play when you've never had a childhood? It felt impossible. It's like asking a blind person to explain the colour of the sky. While I was struggling to mother my inner child, my son was forced to parent me. History repeating itself, just in a new costume.

My crash didn't create the hunger; it only exposed it as the gapping soul wound it was. It amplified the gnawing emptiness I'd lived with all my life, but for the first time, I couldn't outrun it anymore. I had to stand in my power and face it head-on, not only to become a better example for my son but to finally embrace my inner child and fight for my own sense of worth.

The Forge

At my core, I believed love meant sacrifice. I thought I had to set myself on fire to keep others warm, to prove my loyalty and show I could be trusted. I stayed, forgave him again and again – not because the hurt stopped but because I wanted to prove I'd never abandon him. I convinced myself it was my job to ease his fears.

But the truth? Each time I stayed and allowed my boundaries to be obliterated, the only one I abandoned was myself. I silenced my inner child – the girl who stayed quiet to protect her mum, who believed I was responsible for how I influenced people's urges, that my pain was punishment, who thought suffering was the only way to prove I was worthy of connection, of God's love, or anyone's love for that matter. But that wasn't love, it was self-abandonment and the cruellest cycle and illusion of all. Burning myself down, not to light the way for others but to convince myself I deserved to exist at all.

The hunger, the crash, the aftermath – they all pushed me into the forge. FIRE became my teacher. This is where the shift had to happen, because survival is not love. Forgiveness is not love if it comes at the cost of yourself. Self-abandonment is not loyalty. It's self-destruction.

Healing meant more than recovering my body. It meant facing the voices that lived inside my head – the ones I'd swallowed without question my whole life. They were like outdated food shoved to the back of a deep cupboard. At one time, they may have kept me alive. But now they'd gone mouldy, rancid and toxic because I'd come from scarcity. I metaphorically closed my eyes to the reality and ate them anyway. I consumed their poison like it was all I deserved.

My son became the beacon in the smoke. When I couldn't breathe, when the guilt and shame felt suffocating, he was the light that forced me forward. If I couldn't rise for myself, I had to rise for him. It was the same reason I'd left a violent relationship years before – not because I suddenly believed I deserved better but because I knew he did. He needed better. That love, that protection – I could give to him, and I must (even when I still denied it to myself). But the truth I had to learn was that what I thought was love wasn't love. It was self-abandonment. It was staying small, burning myself down, twisting myself into someone else's comfort because I didn't think I was worthy of anything more.

That's when the forge began. Not just surviving but learning to thrive. To question the voices, to break the rules that were killing me. To finally ignite the truth of who I was. The accident forced me to stop. To face everything I'd been outrunning. The shame, the fear, the lies I'd believed about responsibility and worth. As much as it burned, it was the forge I needed because there's no more pretending and no more outrunning when you finally face the fire head-on.

And that's how the FIRE Liberation Fingerprint™ was born.

This was more than an idea or theory; it was my survival and my rebirth. FIRE was an acronym for my journey of discovery and finding my identity and aligning with my truth.

F for Face the Flame

I for Identify and Ignite

R for Release, Rewire and Rewrite

E for Embody (and become the Example)

Remember, you don't need to rebuild everything at once. FIRE is both a destroyer and a forge. Start with sparks. Let them catch. Let them burn. Because you are 'Too Lit to Quit' too!

Twee Shaw *is a solo mum, speaker and founder of* The FIRE Revolution – *a global movement helping women rise from what tried to burn them to become the FIRE.*

A Vietnamese boat refugee and survivor of childhood, sexual and domestic violence, and shaped by adversity of complex PTSD, chronic illness and a near-fatal car crash, Twee transformed her pain into purpose through her signature FIRE Liberation Fingerprint™. *As a dynamic speaker, author and mentor, Twee is known for her unstoppable energy, raw honesty and rally cry: Too Lit to Quit!*

At home, she's raising her nine-year-old neuro-spicy sidekick (part Young Sheldon, *part Ma-Ti from* Captain Planet*), already planning his own kids' revolution rising as a lighthouse for others.*

Purpose, Power and Becoming

Laying the Foundations of a Dream Life

Cecilia Huang

For over twelve years, I journeyed through the world of B2B marketing, crafting strategies, meeting goals and ticking off achievements. But deep down, I knew my true calling lived beyond corporate key performance indicators (KPIs) and campaign briefs. My heart was tugging me towards something more human, more soulful.

The leap that changed my life forever wasn't dramatic. It began one ordinary Sunday night, at 3:00 am. I woke up, gripped by anxiety, already dreading the tasks that awaited me at work. That moment of restlessness became a turning point. I began asking myself if this was it? Was this the life I wanted to live?

That single moment planted the seed for change. I started exploring how to build habits that could sustain not just productivity, but positivity. How could I move through the week with a sense of meaning, not just relief on Fridays? That quiet questioning turned into a mission: to inspire and support other working people to live their dream lives, not just on weekends or holidays, but in the ordinary, in-between moments of every day.

I believe happiness isn't something we wait for; it's something we cultivate. Through small, intentional acts, we can shift our mindset, reconnect with our purpose and slowly, meaningfully, transform our lives from the inside out.

Leaving behind the conventional path, I began writing. I poured my thoughts into books and journals, sharing ideas on self-love, purpose and the power of daily rituals. I shared personal stories, habits and affirmations – the tools that helped me rediscover my voice and align with my values. My dream became clear: to help others reconnect with theirs.

To me, living a dream life is not about chasing grand success, it's about uncovering your why and learning how to live it, day by day. It's about imagining a life where joy isn't reserved for TGIF but woven into the fabric of Monday through Sunday. It's about waking up with intention, finding beauty in the small things and celebrating progress, even in the quietest moments.

Through my journey, I've learned to see 'failures', 'regrets' and even the messy, weird chapters as necessary parts of the story. They shaped the woman I am today. And now, I write to remind others: your past doesn't define you; it refines you.

This leap from corporate strategist to soulful storyteller wasn't just a career change. It was a reclamation of purpose. Today, I guide others through words of empowerment, daily reminders and gentle encouragement, helping them reconnect with their dreams, their truth and themselves.

Facing the Inner Critics

The leap that changed my life didn't come without resistance, instead, it came after wrestling with some of the most difficult emotions I've ever had to face: fear, self-sabotage and perfectionism. Each one had its grip on me in different ways, quietly shaping how I saw myself, what I believed I was capable of and whether I was 'allowed' to dream bigger.

The first emotion to strike was fear. It shows up for so many of us. Sometimes disguised as doubt, hesitation or even overthinking. For me, it was a mix of fear of failure, fear of making the wrong move and, ironically, even fear of success. I've changed jobs more than twenty times throughout my career. Each time I handed in my resignation, especially during the notice period, doubt would creep in. Is this the right move? What if I don't like the next job? Am I just running away? Fear of the unknown made me second-guess my own intuition.

Then there was self-sabotage, that quiet, invisible force that slowly chipped away at my confidence. It often wore clever disguises: 'I'm just being realistic' or 'I'm not quite ready yet'. Looking back, I can name the moments I delayed starting something meaningful, questioned my abilities or shied away from decisions that truly aligned with my heart. At the time, I couldn't see it clearly. That's the tricky thing about self-sabotage – it doesn't shout. It whispers, 'You're not ready. You're not enough. Someone else is already doing it better.'

The hardest part is how it sneaks into routine, becoming a familiar pattern. Without realising, I leaned into perfectionism, telling myself that everything had to be flawless before I could begin. That mindset gave me the illusion of control, but in truth, it was holding me back.

Perfectionism, though often praised as a strength, was quietly draining the joy from my creative process. I placed impossibly high expectations on myself, tying my worth to how polished or perfect things looked. If something wasn't just right, it didn't feel worthy of being shared. I'd delay, rewrite, overthink or sometimes abandon it altogether. That inner critic, the one that constantly whispers do more, be more and be better, left me running on empty.

It kept me in my comfort zone, afraid to try new things unless I could master them immediately. It stopped me from embracing failure, which is actually where the deepest learning happens. It made me procrastinate, waiting for the perfect time or the perfect idea before starting. It left me feeling not enough, relying on external validation to feel worthy. It fuelled constant anxiety, with an inner voice that never let me rest or celebrate progress.

All of this – the fear, the self-sabotage, the perfectionism – created a loop that kept me chasing safety instead of purpose. And yet, the moment I decided to leap, I wasn't fearless, I was simply ready to stop letting fear have the final say.

Stepping Beyond the Comfort Zone

I didn't overcome my fears in one defining moment. There was no grand epiphany, just a quiet decision to start. To write, create and share, even when I was afraid. Especially when it wasn't perfect.

I began to redefine success, not as flawless outcomes or external validation, but as showing up with heart, staying true to my values and following my curiosity. I stopped waiting to be ready and started trusting that progress, not perfection, was enough.

The first real sign I was on the right path came not in applause or big wins, but in something much smaller: a sense of alignment. For the first time in years, I felt like I was finally listening to myself. The anxiety that used to accompany every Sunday night began to soften. I still felt scared, but I was no longer paralysed by it. Instead, I began to respond to my fear with gentle awareness, learning to see it not as a barrier, but a sign that I was growing.

Learning to Live Beyond the Comfort Zone

For years, I felt stuck between wanting more and fearing the cost of change. I began to gently explore what lived beyond the boundaries of my comfort zone.

One exercise that helped was simply drawing a circle. Inside, I wrote the things I felt safe with – routine tasks, familiar habits, known environments. Outside, I listed the things that made me uncomfortable – networking, starting something new, expressing vulnerability. This small act helped me name my fears, rather than be ruled by them.

From there, I began taking small, deliberate steps. When I noticed fear creeping in, I'd ask myself: What am I really afraid of here? Sometimes it was rejection, sometimes failure, sometimes the fear of being seen trying. I didn't have to conquer those feelings overnight. I just had to face them, one at a time.

Baby Steps Became Breakthroughs

Stepping out of my comfort zone didn't mean taking a giant leap into the unknown. For me, it looked more like lingering a little longer in the discomfort, staying in a conversation when I wanted to retreat, pressing 'post' on words I'd rewritten a dozen times, even when my inner critic whispered, 'not good enough'. Over time, those small, quiet acts of courage began to build something stronger: trust in myself.

And when I failed – because I did and still do – I began to treat failure not as a verdict, but as a teacher. It wasn't easy at first. Every misstep felt personal, like proof I wasn't cut out for the path I'd chosen. But slowly, I started to shift my perspective. I reminded myself, again and again, that failure isn't the opposite of success, but is woven into the journey towards it.

What helped most was knowing I wasn't alone. I began reading the stories of others, those women who'd stumbled, restarted, pivoted and grown. Their honesty gave me permission to embrace my own imperfections. I realised no-one's path is a straight line. We just don't always see the messy drafts, the quiet doubts, or the behind-the-scenes moments of resilience. And that's okay. The messiness is what makes the story real.

Inner Shifts and Everyday Signs

Some of the most powerful signs that I was on the right path were the quietest.

Feeling grateful for tiny things at the end of the day, like the warmth of a cup of tea, the softness of a page turning in a notebook. In these quiet moments, I discovered my courage to say, "This may not be perfect, but it matters to me, and that's enough." I also started letting go of perfectionism, which had kept me stuck in cycles of procrastination and self-doubt. I realised that perfectionism had less to do with high standards and more to do with fear – of not being enough and of what others might think. The more I gave myself permission to be imperfect, the more I began to thrive.

The Most Important Sign: Belief

At some point, something shifted. I began to believe that change wasn't just a faraway idea, but something I could reach for, touch and live. That belief didn't come from applause, external validation or any big breakthrough. It came quietly from the inside out, built through the small act of showing up for myself, even when it felt hard and even when the progress felt invisible.

I began to believe that I could learn, grow and become the person I'd always dreamed of being. Not by waiting for the perfect moment or making one bold leap, but by honouring the daily choices that added up over time. I whispered to myself often: You don't need to leap. You can walk gently towards your dream, one small step at a time.

And somewhere along that walk, I started to have fun. I let myself laugh at the missteps, delight in the detours and soften into the process of becoming. I allowed myself to feel joy, even in the uncertainty. Not just the kind of joy that arrives with milestones, but the quiet, steady joy of knowing I was finally on my path.

That's when I knew: I was getting closer to the life I was meant to live; I felt more like *me*.

Turning Challenges into Stepping Stones

To be honest, I put off writing my first book for almost a year.

Every time I sat down to write, life found a way to pull me away – urgent emails, increased workload, laptop malfunctions, a sudden fire alarm in my building. There was always something. But looking back now, I realise it wasn't just life's logistics getting in the way. It was fear. Fear of not being good enough. Fear that my words wouldn't matter. Fear that my story wasn't worth telling.

After a year of circling around the idea, I stopped waiting for the perfect moment. I've lived long enough to feel how quickly the days pass; how easy it is to lose sight of who I am in the middle of it all. But I've come to realise that this chapter of life is a beautiful beginning, writing became the way I found my way back home to myself. I created a system that helped me commit, even on messy days. I'm sharing it here; in case you need a gentle nudge too.

Set Your Intention

Clarity is power. I began each day by setting a quiet, soulful intention, not just 'I want to write' but *why* I wanted to write. What story needed to be told? What part of me was ready to speak?

This daily ritual became a compass. Even when I had to pause for work or family or life's curveballs, I could return to that inner 'why' and find my footing again.

Take One Step at a Time

Writing a book can feel like climbing a mountain barefoot, especially when you're balancing a full life. I quickly learned to break everything into tiny, manageable steps.

Sometimes, all I needed to do was open my laptop and sit with my thoughts. I followed what I call the 'Two-Minute Rule': start with something that takes no more than two minutes. Light a candle. Write one sentence. Organise my notes. The magic lies in starting small and staying consistent. You don't need a marathon session, but just a moment of commitment.

Make It Convenient

As women in midlife, we're often managing homes, jobs, partnerships, aging parents or even teenagers. Time can feel like a luxury. So, I made writing convenient. I created a corner in my home that felt inspiring, kept a notebook beside my bed and sometimes dictated notes into my phone while on a walk. I stopped romanticising productivity and instead embraced progress in whatever form it took.

Build a Tribe

This is perhaps the most powerful thing I did. I surrounded myself with people who were also in the process of creating, healing, sharing and dreaming. Friends who understood the vulnerability of starting over, the courage it takes to show up and the joy of rooting for one another.

There's something deeply affirming about being part of a circle of people who are no longer trying to prove themselves but are instead committed to living with intention and purpose. When you walk alongside others who believe in your growth, you stop doubting whether you belong.

Writing that first book wasn't just about publishing a manuscript. It was about reclaiming a voice I'd silenced for too long. It was about making peace with imperfection, trusting the timing of my own unfolding and realising that my story mattered, simply because it was mine.

I published my first book, *The Dream Life Project*, in April 2024 to help others explore the power of their dreams, deciphering their hidden messages, embracing their transformative potential and uncovering the passions that lie within. The book is a gentle guide to overcoming limitations and igniting a sense of purpose. It invites readers to trust the wisdom of their dreams and take inspired action, knowing those dreams can lead them towards a more meaningful, fulfilling, and purpose-driven life.

In December 2024, I released a three-book series designed to inspire everyday wellbeing and intentional living: *Daily Rituals: 101 Small*

Acts to Unlock Happiness; *Daily Mantras: 101 Little Ways to Spark Joy*; and *Daily Practices: 101 Tiny Steps to Reclaim Compassion*.

A growing community has blossomed on my Instagram, where over 3,800 kindred spirits gather to embrace a gentler, more intentional way of living. Each day, I share words that invite reflection, nurture self-discovery and rekindle love for self and for life.

It fills my heart to hear from followers who've made these daily notes part of their morning rituals: setting intentions, finding calm and choosing to live with purpose. Together, we're building quiet, meaningful lives, one dreamy reminder at a time.

The Ripple Effect of Courage

One of the most unexpected gifts of my leap has been the ripple effect it's created around me. Friends, colleagues and even strangers on the internet have told me how my journey sparked something in them, whether it was starting a journal, launching a side project or simply showing up for themselves with more intention. When I began sharing my story honestly, imperfectly and from the heart, I gave others permission to do the same.

Some told me they'd been stuck in the same job for years, afraid to take the first step. After hearing my story, they started exploring new paths, even if just in their minds. Others began practising small rituals of self-love: journalling, daily affirmations, writing down dreams they hadn't dared speak aloud. That's the power of lived experience; it creates a mirror for others to see what's possible for themselves.

I like to say that your destiny might be written but the path you take is your choice. We might not be able to control every outcome but we can choose how we show up, how we dream and how we grow.

Shifting the Mindset from 'Someday' to 'Now'

One message I always come back to is this: stop postponing happiness. So many of us say, "I'll be happy when..." When I get that promotion. When I find a partner. When I buy a house. But if we wait for everything to fall into place, we miss the beauty of the present.

Instead, I encourage others.

Measure success against your own progress, not a distant ideal.

Celebrate the little wins – a small habit kept, a new idea explored, a single page written.

Dream bigger, not for the outcome, but for who you become in the process.

Be kind to yourself, especially when progress is slow or uncertain.

Building Habits, One Small Step at a Time

A few friends told me they felt stuck in a rut – doing the same thing every day, feeling uninspired.

I've been there.

What helped me was starting small: changing my routine, listening to a new podcast, creating something just for fun. These tiny changes created new energy and I began to feel like I was reclaiming my own story. Now, I see others doing the same, adding joy and intention to their lives.

The Little Ways I Inspire, Without Realising

A colleague once said, "Watching you build your own path reminded me I could still build mine." Another friend started writing again after years of putting it off. Not because I told her to, but because she saw me doing it, even when she had every reason not to.

It's never about being perfect. It's about being real. I show people that they don't have to have it all figured out. They just have to start.

Creating Space for Others to Dream

By sharing what's worked for me, like journalling gratitude, breaking big dreams into small actions and checking in with myself regularly, I've helped others feel less overwhelmed and more empowered. I encourage people to: track progress over perfection; build new habits gradually; focus on strengths instead of shortcomings; and set goals rooted in purpose, not pressure.

When we live with intention, we naturally invite others to do the same.

In the end, I didn't set out to 'inspire' others. I set out to save myself from a life of going through the motions. But what I've learned is this: when you choose courage, others often find theirs too. When you share your story, you give others permission to tell theirs.

A Letter to My Younger Self

If I could go back to before I jumped – the one who lay awake at night wondering if there was more to life than deadlines, detachment and doing it all – I'd sit beside her gently and say: "This leap you're about to take won't be clean. It won't be perfect. It won't look like the highlight reels you scroll past. But it will be the beginning of your becoming. Trust it."

Before the leap, I would've loved someone to remind me of this simple truth: you don't need to have it all figured out. You just need to know who you are becoming matters more than any destination. That alone is enough reason to begin.

I'd tell her to get to know herself, really know herself. Not the version that showed up for performance reviews or replied to emails at midnight. But the version who feels alive when writing, who lights up when creating, who's allowed to want things for herself, not just for others. I'd say: "You're allowed to want joy, meaning and a slower, richer life. Wanting that doesn't make you selfish, it makes you human."

I'd tell her: set boundaries, say no when you need to. Protect your energy like it's sacred, because it is. I'd remind her not to compare herself to others. Their success doesn't diminish hers. Their paths are different, not better.

If I could whisper anything into her ear, it would be this: "You don't have to be perfect to be worthy. You don't need permission to begin. And your value was never up for debate."

Now that I've made the jump, I can see that building a dream life is part mindset, part habit. So, I'd also give her some practical truths.

Write your goals down – dreams are clearer when they're on paper. Declutter your mind and your space; let go of what's no longer yours to carry. Start small – don't chase the mountain; take one step. Prioritise your health – it's not indulgent, it's foundational. Celebrate tiny wins because progress often looks like quiet consistency, not big applause.

I'd tell her that failure is not fatal, it's a teacher. That fear is just a sign you're growing. That some people won't understand your decision – and that's okay. You're not here to live someone else's dream.

And finally, I'd say this:

Please be kind to yourself. Speak to yourself like someone you love. You're going to make mistakes, lots of them. That's not weakness, that's humanity.

The truth is, you'll still feel fear. You'll still battle perfectionism and uncertainty. But now you'll have tools. You'll build rituals. You'll remember your why. You'll become your own safe place. And as you walk this path, you'll light the way for others too. You don't need to be confident to leap, you just need to be committed.

If I could go back and sit beside that version of me again, I'd hold her hand and say, "You're going to be okay. In fact, you're going to bloom."

To any woman reading this who has put off her dreams, her words, or her next brave step: this is your reminder that it's never too late. Not at forty, not at fifty, not at seventy. You are not behind. You are right on time.

Start where you are. One sentence. One breath. One brave act at a time. The world needs your story and more importantly, **you** deserve to tell it.

For over twelve years, **Cecilia Huang** *journeyed through the world of B2B marketing, but her true calling extends far beyond corporate strategies and business goals, her heart lies in empowering and uplifting those who are striving to find balance and meaning in the midst of their busy lives.*

Cecilia believes that happiness isn't something reserved for the weekend or special occasions; it's something we can cultivate daily through small, intentional acts. Her writing is born from a deep desire to help others find happiness, to remind them that every day is an opportunity to connect with their inner selves.

Dance Like the World's Not Closing - Even If It Is

Adelle Givney

Sitting in the middle of the sixth row, I turned to look at my husband. We couldn't wipe the smiles off our faces. Looking up at the screens on either side of the stage, we grabbed each other's arms when we saw our daughter's photo and bio appear. Tears spilled over as I took a deep breath. Finally. Finally, we were there to watch her dance on her home away from home on the other side of the world aboard a beautiful cruise ship. It felt surreal. Dreamlike. I kept expecting to wake up. Eventually the lights went down, the music swelled and the show began.

I'd been a 'dance mum' since Molly turned five and started at a local dance school on a Saturday morning. One ballet, jazz and tap class turned into more classes, eisteddfods, exams, solos and concerts. Before we knew it, she was finishing high school and moving interstate to undertake a two-year full-time dance program. Because she was still young, I left my job, and my husband and older sons stayed in Brisbane while she and I moved to Melbourne. The two years flew by, with shows and auditions taking place while we also played tourist.

Returning to Brisbane, she'd made it to the end of several auditions, including cruise ships and Moulin Rouge. Now came the waiting game. She had a job and took dance classes while waiting for the life-changing contract to hit her inbox.

In February 2020 – can you guess where I'm going here? – that email finally arrived from a cruise ship company. A contract on one of their ships, starting training in the US in May. While I had a nagging in the back of my mind about this new flu going around, we were so excited and proud. We'd definitely be going to watch her and see some of the world – a dream come true!

Almost without warning, Covid-19 escalated and the world shut down. The contract was pushed back, but the cruise line assured her it would still be going ahead – they just weren't sure when.

We watched as dancing friends and colleagues lost their jobs, contracts and way of life. They were stranded on cruise ships, sailing to nowhere and crowded in staff quarters in places like Tokyo, Shanghai and Miami. They trickled back to Australia, spending weeks in isolation in hotels before they could return home. Stage shows were postponed or outright cancelled.

As time went on, dance schools went online and loungerooms, garages, bedrooms, kitchens and bathrooms became impromptu studios. Pets joined the Zoom calls, and hilarity ensued. Dancers could access dance classes from around the world – often getting up before sunrise to pull on their leggings and crop tops and set up their laptops or phones. Other house members were woken to rhythmic thumps and jumps; sometimes candlesticks tumbled from shelves onto the floor – true story!

Dancers and the arts were low down on the priority for payments and financial assistance. Many had no income at all, and with usual employment industries like hospitality all but closed down, there were little to no options for employment.

Molly wanted to bolster everyone's spirits. She had an idea – a collaboration that would involve as many dancers as wanted to take part. She reached out and the response was overwhelming: fifty-two elite, professional dancers from around the world wanted to be involved!

She started by choosing music and choreographing a short piece for herself. She filmed it and then sent that to the next dancer – a young New Zealander in isolation at Tokyo Disney – who took up where she left off and then sent it back. It was then sent to a contemporary dancer in isolation in Melbourne, who followed on – and so on and so forth.

The project involved dancers from six different cruise lines, San Francisco Ballet company, New Zealand Ballet, dance studios, Queensland University of Technology, Western Australia Academy of Performing Arts – with many also having danced overseas in highly regarded places such as Moulin Rouge and with the Rockettes.

After many hours of editing, the finished product was uploaded to YouTube and shared via social media. What happened next took us completely by surprise. It went viral. Not just locally but worldwide! It was picked up by news outlets and television studios. Molly was featured in national newspapers, spotlighted by global social media groups and interviewed live on the Sunday edition of *Sunrise*. It was incredible and was just what the dance world needed.

The world slowly started to reopen and Molly received a new contract offer from a different ship and itinerary – The Mediterranean. Despite delays and shifting start dates, it was finally happening!

Usually, the cast met in the rehearsal studios in the US, but with quarantine requirements, they flew to Cyprus and spent two weeks in isolation before joining the ship, where they would then spend another two weeks in quarantine before learning and then installing the shows.

There were only thirty-six people on her flight to Cyprus. When they all arrived, they were ferried to the hotel where they spent the next two weeks alone. Thankfully, Facetime helped connect during isolation. Despite the time difference, family and friends rallied to keep her spirits up.

After the two weeks on Cyprus, they signed on the ship and were in guest cabins with balconies. Now began the next two weeks of quarantine, with food being delivered three times a day to their cabins.

"Mum, did you pack any cold and flu tablets?"

My heart jumped when I read this message. She'd developed symptoms – headache, runny nose and sore throat. I told her that she should let her Dance Captain (DC) know, which she did.

Medical came and performed a rapid test. And then another.

I was FaceTiming her when she got a call saying that it was positive.

She was moved into an interior room with no balcony that night, and they followed up with a polymerase chain reaction (PCR) test that confirmed Covid-19 a few days later.

This is where the real trouble began.

The cruise line had to report a positive Covid case on board and Molly was advised she'd need to be disembarked. Wearing a full hazmat suit, she was taken off the ship by a small boat, transferred into an ambulance on the dock, and driven away.

She was taken to a quarantine hotel – quite ironically named *Eden* – where, unbelievably, everyone who'd tested positive was quarantined *together*, not separately. This was so different to how Covid was managed in Australia.

She was told she may be sharing a room. Keep in mind, she was just twenty-one years old, Australian, and this was her first time away from home. She rang me in tears. When she got to her room, the door wouldn't even close, let alone lock. People were wandering the halls. As her mum, sitting helplessly on the other side of the world, it was terrifying.

Looking out the window, she could even see prisoners, presumably Covid positive, in handcuffs being led inside.

That's when I stepped in.

I contacted the ship's executive and made sure to use the words *young*, *safety* and *duty of care*, more than once. The ambulance crew had already contacted the Cyprus police, who then contacted the Australian Embassy. They rang Eden to speak to Molly. I had to laugh; Molly was genuinely surprised they were Australian.

That night, I spent hours on the phone with the shoreside medical team, the ship's executive officer, Robert, and, of course, Molly. The cruise line sent their Cyprus port contact to Eden to fix Molly's door so she could at least lock it. I was beyond grateful. By then it was 2 am in Australia, and I told her I'd try to get a few hours' sleep.

Two hours later, I woke to incredible news.

Another crew member from the IT team had also tested positive while in the hotel and hadn't made it onto the ship. She'd already been at Eden for a week.

The cruise line executive arranged alternative accommodation for them: a house in the hills of Cyprus, just outside a small village. It was like something out of a movie. Fully catered, they called their daily menu orders in to the local taverna each morning.

They stayed there for a week. Molly even rehearsed out on the front lawn via Zoom. I can only imagine what the neighbours thought.

Then, with just thirty minutes' warning, they were told to pack everything up. They were being transferred back to the dock to rejoin the ship.

The other girl, having completed more than two weeks of quarantine, passed through immigration and boarded successfully.

But when Molly tried, the Cyprus government and health department refused to let her through. They screamed at her, called the police and flatly denied her entry even though the ship was ready and waiting to take her back.

Cue the next horrendous situation.

I was crying. She was crying. I was terrified they were going to send her all the way back to *Eden*. I got back on the phone to the ship's executive team, who were just as concerned as I was. Thankfully, they managed to arrange for Molly to be taken instead to the original hotel she'd stayed in and they took pity on her. They gave her a room with a separate bedroom, and even a balcony.

It was a small win in the middle of a very stressful mess.

The next hurdle? The ship wasn't even docked when her isolation technically ended. So, we waited. And waited.

Then, just when things seemed to be settling down, civil war broke out in Israel.

Israel was meant to be the ship's home port, where passengers would be picked up. More changes.

On Saturday, with just fifteen minutes' notice, Molly got a call: a taxi was on its way to collect her.

Luckily, she'd packed and was ready.

She met her ship agent at the dock, the same lovely man who'd dropped off a care package of chips, chocolate and biscuits for her during her isolation.

Finally, she was taken straight through immigration and onto the ship.

It was around 7 pm here. We were at a friend's house with a group when her message came through. I burst into tears and there were cheers all around.

Due to the war in Israel, the ship had to change itinerary and return to port from the US. They arranged a crew swap with another ship as US visas were required. Thankfully, Molly had one, but a few dancers didn't and had to return home to organise theirs, with plans to rejoin the ship later.

While in the required two-week quarantine onboard – again – Molly rehearsed daily in her cabin. She stayed fit, focused and performance-ready. The install team and IT department even set up a live stream of the rehearsals on one of the staff TV channels, which was the first time anything like that had ever been done and it actually made the cruise line news. It was extraordinary.

Two long weeks later, Molly was out of quarantine and able to join the rest of her cast. Adhering to health protocols, everyone wore face masks as rehearsals began.

Initially there were no passengers on board, and so the crew had access to guest areas. The shows were finally installed, and the cast settled into the rhythm of ship life. The dancers and singers were starting to build friendships.

Of course, as anyone who lived through 2021 knows, that wasn't the end. There was more quarantine, extra layers of precaution, rigorous health rules to limit exposure – to be honest, I never knew what messages and photos I'd be waking up to every morning. But Molly was on a ship, dancing professionally and growing up fast.

The next nine months were filled with dancing to slowly increasing audience numbers, along with more rounds of quarantine as the dreaded 'close contact' or even 'positive PCR' occurred. The inevitable 're-block' due to that quarantine to adjust for missing cast occurred.

Finally, things started to shift, and Molly was finally able to step off the ship and explore some of the beautiful Caribbean Islands. This was what she – and I – had been waiting for.

By the end of her contract, Molly had spent ninety days in quarantine – at that stage the most of any crew member!

She was asked to extend her contract to assist with the next cast install. When that was completed, she was on a long flight home, wearing a mask the whole way. She landed in Sydney and then had to wait to get a connecting flight to Brisbane.

I think I was at the airport before she even took off!

To see her walk towards me was everything, and many, many tears were shed. There's nothing like folding your child into your arms after all that time apart and the challenges she'd faced. It was long overdue, and I never wanted to let her go.

In April 2022, Molly accepted a contract with Rhonda Burchmore, performing as a showgirl in both Brisbane and Sydney. Naturally I went to shows in both cities, as all good dance mums should.

It was fantastic to see her in her heels and feathers again; it had been so long.

A few months later she woke to a new contract in her inbox from the cruise line. She decided to accept this one, and plans began.

She left in August, this time flying to the US to rehearse the shows before installing on the ship. What a completely different experience!

There were still weekly PCR tests, and Covid still made the occasional, unwanted appearance, but it was far better than the uncertainty of the year before.

This time, we knew we had to go cruising ourselves, so we made plans.

Because it was so far away from Australia, we planned four back-to-back cruises, including a Caribbean Cruise, a Transatlantic crossing and two Mediterranean itineraries. I think people thought we were a bit crazy! Forty-two nights in total, after only ever being on one seven-night cruise many years ago. It seemed to take forever for April to arrive, but eventually we were on our way.

Those four weeks onboard were some of the most amazing days of my life.

We spent time with Molly, met her wonderful cast and became their honorary 'dance parents' as well. We explored Europe together for the first time and visited some incredible and truly breathtaking places. Santorini, Mykonos, Miracle Square and Valencia were among our favourites. We even had a day in Cyprus, which – I'm not going to lie – was a bit triggering.

But nothing – *NOTHING* - beat sitting in that beautiful theatre and watching her strut her stuff.

In those final moments of the show, as the curtain fell, the applause roared and we surged to our feet, it hit me: we survived all of it. The PCRs, the panicked phone calls, the lockdowns, the distance. We danced through the chaos in our own way.

And now, every time I see her on a stage, I don't just see a dancer. I see strength, joy and the rhythm of a life being lived to the fullest.

Adelle Givney *is a proud Brisbane-based dance mum who has survived eisteddfods, feathered costumes, last-minute rehearsals, and a global pandemic — all in support of her daughter's international dance career. From suburban studios to cruise ship stages on the other side of the world, Adelle has cheered (and occasionally wept) from the wings, the sixth row, and just about every kind of departure gate imaginable.*

A lifelong dance mum turned cruise-ship-contract crisis manager, Adelle now channels those same survival skills into educating adults – with only slightly fewer sequins involved. Her background as an adult educator helped equip her for the logistical gymnastics required to manage contract delays, emergency repatriations, midnight embassy calls and emotionally fraught packing lists. She's earned an unofficial PhD in patience (with a minor in crisis triage and expert-level panic management).

The Phoenix Within: Rising from the Ashes

Elena Saikova

There's a moment in every woman's life where she stands at a crossroads: one road familiar but suffocating, the other unknown but promising freedom.

For me, that moment came with my son in my arms. He was just a baby, blissfully unaware of the storm I was walking through. My heart was pounding, my legs felt like lead and I made a quiet promise to myself: *I will not let this be my story.*

I still remember the cool evening air on my face as I stepped out the door that day. The pavement under my shoes felt unfamiliar, as though I was stepping into a different country altogether. My senses were heightened with every sound, every breath and every heartbeat, as if my body knew this was not just another walk. This was the first step into a different life.

My fingers gripped the strap of my bag until they ached, and my other arm cradled my son's soft body close to my chest. His head nestled against me; the steady rhythm of his breathing was both a comfort and a reminder of the life I needed to protect.

I left my home, my belongings and the life I thought I was supposed to have. What I didn't realise then was that I was also leaving behind an old version of myself, the one who'd learned to survive but had forgotten how to truly live.

The First Steps

Our first night in the new place was quiet except for the hum of the fridge. It was smaller, colder, unfamiliar. The mattress was low to the floor, and long after my son fell asleep beside me, I lay awake, listening to the distant sounds of traffic and wondering if I'd made the biggest mistake of my life.

But in the morning, sunlight spilled across the walls like it was trying to tell me something: *You made it to another day.*

The days that followed were raw. Life was stripped back to its bare essentials. Feeding my son, keeping us safe and trying to keep my own head above water became my entire world. Each night, when he finally fell asleep, the weight of my exhaustion pressed down hard. But beneath the fatigue, a small ember flickered within me steady, unyielding, whispering: *This is not where your story ends.*

I remember sitting by the window one chilly morning, wrapped in a soft blanket, watching the world wake. The pale light filtered through the trees, and for a moment it felt like the first breath of something new. The air smelled like rain on dry earth – fresh, hopeful.

I did not know then how long the road ahead would be, but I knew I had to hold on to that ember. It was my quiet rebellion against despair. It was the promise that no matter how dark things became, the dawn would come.

The Fire That Forged Me

What followed was a legal battle that tested every part of me. It was intense, expensive and often brutal – a trial not just in court, but within me.

I faced endless courtrooms, crossed paths with barristers wielding words like weapons and watched as the financial cost mounted, threatening to crush my spirit. Every document I filed, every cross-examination I endured chipped away at the woman I used to be and forced me to discover a stronger, clearer voice hidden beneath the ashes.

I learned that strength is not loud. It's not about grand gestures or heroic victories. Sometimes it's just showing up again the next day. Sometimes it's holding on when every part of you wants to let go.

When it finally ended, I was left with a new kind of emptiness – not just a bank account drained, but an emotional hollow that whispered: *Now what?*

The Climb

I began to notice the little victories. The first time I handled a difficult situation on my own and felt proud instead of afraid. The first time I laughed – really laughed – and realised it had been months since my shoulders felt that light. The first time I looked in the mirror and saw not the woman who'd been through heartbreak, but the woman who was building something new from the ground up.

Some days, that spark inside me roared into a flame. I started imagining a future where my life was not defined by what I'd left behind, but by what I was creating. I didn't know exactly what it looked like yet, but I knew it had colour, light and strength in it.

It was not all smooth. There were days I felt like I was pushing a boulder uphill. But I began to understand something powerful: resilience is not about never falling; it's about building the muscle to rise again and again.

And rise I did.

There was a night I remember clearly, sitting at the kitchen table after my son was asleep. Papers were spread out in front of me, and the weight of the next steps pressed down like a storm cloud.

Then I thought about the women I'd met in the weeks before, the ones who'd walked through their own fire and came out stronger. And I realised that every single one of them carried the same look in their eyes. It wasn't just survival. It was victory.

That night, something shifted in me. I knew I didn't just want to get through my situation. I wanted to rise. I wanted to turn this pain into something that could light the way for other women.

So, I started to dream differently. I began taking small, steady steps towards a future that was not just about getting by, but about creating a life I could be proud of.

The Quiet Decision

The answer didn't come as a lightning bolt. It came quietly in the form of a decision I almost didn't make: to go back to university.

At the time, I was exhausted. I was already working and navigating single motherhood. The thought of studying again felt overwhelming, almost impossible. But I knew deep down that I had to build something new, something stronger.

At first, it was quiet like a seed pushing through soil. I began to dream bigger. I enrolled to study law, chasing the qualification that had once seemed impossible.

Deep down, I knew I wanted to help women like me who were navigating life's most brutal storms. I wanted to stand with them – not just as someone who understood the law, but as someone who understood them.

Those years were a blur of textbooks and late-night study sessions. My kitchen table was permanently buried under case notes and highlighters. There were nights I teared up over a keyboard, questioning my sanity. But every subject I passed and every assignment I submitted were bricks in the foundation of the life I was creating.

The hours were long, the work intense and the balancing act of motherhood and study felt like juggling fire. But every late night and early morning became fuel. My *why* was stronger than any obstacle: I wanted to be the woman I'd needed back then. I wanted to be a guide, a sister and a voice saying: *You can do this. You are not alone.*

Finding Beauty in the Battle

I remember sitting at my tiny kitchen table, the soft glow of my laptop the only light in the room as the city around me settled into sleep. My son's toys lay scattered around, a reminder of why I was doing this. For him.

For a while, my world was all survival. But one afternoon, while walking through the markets, I stopped in front of a stall selling flowers. They weren't practical. They weren't on my shopping list. But the sunflowers were so bright, so unapologetically joyful, that I bought a bunch.

When I placed them in a vase on my kitchen bench, the whole room seemed to change. It was not just about the flowers; it was about remembering that beauty still had a place in my life.

After that, I started looking for it everywhere: the way sunlight caught the steam rising from my morning coffee, the sound of my son's belly laugh, the feel of warm sand under my toes when we went to the beach.

Beauty did not erase the hard days. But it gave me the strength to move through them.

The Power of Sisterhood

Along the way, I discovered something beautiful – the power of sisterhood. Women who'd walked their own hard roads took me by the hand, shared their wisdom and reminded me of my own light when I forgot it was there. We celebrated each other's wins and held each other through the tears. That connection was and still is one of the richest treasures of my life.

The day I graduated, my son sat in the audience, his little legs swinging, his smile beaming. In that moment, everything came full circle. That tiny baby I carried at the crossroads was now watching his mother walk across a graduation stage, proving to both of us that the unknown road can lead to the most extraordinary destinations.

Shaping Elenix

When I finally qualified as a lawyer, I thought I'd made it. I stepped into the family law world with a heart full of purpose: to help other women like me. But the reality of traditional legal practice did not match my vision. Too much focus on winning battles, not enough on healing hearts. Too much time spent in courtrooms, not enough in creating closure and calm.

I quickly realised that I didn't just want to fight for my clients; I wanted to walk alongside them before the fight even began. To help them find a way through separation that protected their dignity, preserved their peace and safeguarded their futures.

I knew that if I didn't start shaping my work to match my mission, I'd be letting down the woman who left with a baby and a promise. So, I stepped out on my own and opened my own business. That is when Elenix was born. The phoenix in my logo is more than a symbol; it's a story of renewal. Like the phoenix, Elena rises from the ashes, carrying strength born from transformation and hope for what is to come.

When I founded Elenix, I knew it couldn't be just another business. It had to be a sanctuary, a place where women could find both practical solutions and emotional safety. Where they could breathe, gather their strength and make decisions from clarity instead of panic.

But my journey didn't stop there. I went on to qualify as a mediator, deepening my ability to help others not just survive their storms, but find calm seas beyond them. I built my signature program *She Rises with Elenix* as a lighthouse for women navigating separation, so they could steer clear of the rocks and find their own safe harbour.

The phoenix became the heart of my brand because it's more than a symbol, it's a promise.

Lighting the Path for Others

One of the greatest gifts this journey has given me is sisterhood. Women who reach out with stories like mine, stories of heartbreak and hope, loss and liberation. Together, we form a chain of light, each link strong and unbreakable. It's in these connections that the true power of rising lives.

There came a point when women I knew, and some I didn't, began reaching out to me. They'd heard my story, and they wanted to know how I'd done it. How I'd found the courage to leave. How I kept going. How I'd built something new.

Sometimes it was over coffee. Sometimes it was in the aisles of the supermarket. Sometimes it was in a late-night phone call when they just needed to hear someone say, "You'll be okay."

Every time, I told them the truth: it's not easy; it's messy; and it's not instant – but it is worth it and you're stronger than you think.

It felt like the torch had been passed to me and now, I was passing it on.

She Rises Anyway

Every woman's storm is different, but I know this: it will not last forever.

Right now, you might feel like you're walking through fire, but on the other side, you'll carry something no-one can take from you – the unshakable knowledge that you can rise.

To the woman reading this, standing at her own crossroads, I say this: choose the road that leads to your freedom, even if it feels uncertain. Find your sisters. Hold tight to the light ahead.

One day, you'll look back and realise you didn't just survive, you built a life that's yours – entirely and beautifully yours.

This challenging chapter you're in now? It's not the end. It's the part of your story that will make the triumph even sweeter.

When you rise – and you will – you'll see that the fire you walked through did not burn you down. It lit the torch you'll carry for the rest of your life, guiding you and every woman who comes after you towards the light.

The Rise in Motion

The thing about rising is this: it doesn't happen in one big leap. It's a hundred small, deliberate steps. It's deciding, day after day, to take the harder road now so your future self can breathe easier later.

In the early days of rebuilding, my 'rise' didn't look glamorous. It looked like packing school lunches at 6 am, racing to work, juggling deadlines, then studying until midnight. It looked like sitting in my car before walking into lectures, willing myself to stay awake, reminding myself why I was doing this.

Every degree I earned, every qualification I added, were less about the letters after my name and more about reclaiming my power. They were about standing on my own two feet, not just for me but for every woman who would one day sit across from me, wondering if she could survive what she was facing.

The Turning Points

There were moments along the way when everything shifted.

One came during a mediation I was facilitating early in my career. A woman sat across the table, barely speaking, her eyes fixed on the floor. I recognised that look – the look of someone holding themselves together with nothing but sheer will.

I paused the legal talk and asked her softly, "What do you need right now, more than anything?"

She looked up, and for the first time in the session, she spoke clearly: "I need to know this will end. That I won't feel like this forever."

That hit me in the chest. That was me, years earlier. I realised then that my real role was not just to navigate the legal process, it was to help women see the shore when they were drowning.

A Full Circle Moment

Years later, my son and I stood on a hilltop one windy spring afternoon. The grass was dotted with wildflowers, and the air was alive with the scent of freshly cut grass from the park below. He was taller now, his hair whipping into his eyes as he laughed and tried to hold onto his kite.

I stood behind him, watching the kite dance against the sky, a streak of red against endless blue.

It hit me then: we'd made it. The baby I once carried through sleepless nights was now a confident, laughing boy. The fear that had once weighed on me had been replaced with something unshakable; a deep gratitude for the path we'd walked.

He turned, grinning and shouted over the wind, "Mum, look! It's flying higher!"

I smiled, tears pricking my eyes. Yes, I thought. So are we.

Looking Back, Moving Forward

Today, when I look back on that woman who stood at the crossroads with her baby in her arms, I feel nothing but love for her. She didn't know what was ahead, but she stepped forward anyway. She couldn't see the woman she'd become but she trusted enough to begin - and that's what I hope every woman reading this will take with them.

You do not have to have it all figured out before you start.

You do not have to feel fearless before you move.

You just have to take the first step towards the light because on the other side of this chapter in your life is not just freedom, it is joy. It is laughter. It is peace. It is you.

And you are worth every single step it takes to get there.

To Every Woman at Her Crossroads

If you're standing at your own crossroads now with one road familiar but suffocating, and the other unknown but promising freedom, I want you to hear me: choose the road that leads to the light.

It won't always be easy. There will be days you feel like you're stumbling in the dark. But every step forward is a step towards the woman you're meant to become. And along the way, you will find your own sisterhood, women who'll lift you when you falter, who'll remind you that you're more capable, more courageous and more worthy than you can yet imagine.

Your story is not over. In fact, the most beautiful chapters are still ahead. And when you get there, when you feel the sunlight on your face again, you'll know that you didn't just survive.

You rose.

And in doing so, you lit the way for someone else.

The Ripple Effect

When one woman rises, she changes everything around her. Her children see what courage looks like. Her friends feel braver in their own lives. Her workplace notices her confidence. She becomes a living, breathing proof that you can go through hell and come out stronger.

That's why I share my story. Not because I need to relive the pain, but because I know there is a woman reading these words right now who's where I once was; scared, tired, and wondering if she can make it through.

To every woman who reads this: *I see you.*

I see your struggle, your courage, your strength.

The journey is yours, but you're not walking it alone.

Hold on to your promise.

Feed your ember.

And when you're ready, rise.

Every woman's journey is unique, but the power to rise is universal.

I'm living proof that even after leaving everything behind; after walking through fire, you can find joy, purpose, and freedom.

And as you read these words, know this: your light is waiting to shine.

Rise with me.

Elena Saikova *is more than a lawyer and mediator; she is a lifeline for women weathering the storm of separation. Having walked through her own fire with fierce determination to build a better future for her son, she intimately knows the heartbreak, fear, and overwhelming uncertainty that can consume a woman in crisis. But she also knows the profound power of rising.*

Through her signature program, She Rises with Elenix, *Elena guides women from confusion to clarity, from fear to freedom. Blending her legal experience with lived experience and heart-centred wisdom, she helps women find calm, confidence, and closure, focusing on healing solutions beyond courtrooms.*

Do Not Follow What Martha Did and You Will Be Very Successful

Martha Mok

I made every mistake so you don't have to.

If someone told you their greatest success came from getting everything wrong first, you'd probably laugh. I would have too, until I realised that's exactly how I got here.

I've lived through shame, heartbreak, burnout and deep loneliness. I've made impulsive choices, chased love in the wrong places and pushed myself so hard I forgot who I was.

But I didn't stay broken.

This chapter is not a highlight reel. It's a survival guide disguised as a confession.

And if one woman can walk away from this feeling seen – and reminded that it's *not too late* to begin again – then I've done what I came to do.

Lesson 1: The Wrong Right Guy

Sometimes 'till death do us part' feels more like 'till dignity disappears'.

Relationships have always played a big part in my life. From a young age, I craved acceptance, validation and the kind of love that would finally make me feel enough. I thought that if I could just find a man to make me happy, then I'd never feel lonely again.

Sound familiar?

That mindset became the starting point of one of the biggest lessons I've ever had to learn.

Let's rewind to when I was twenty-one. I was supposed to be on a three-month holiday in Hong Kong – just a breather, a little freedom before returning to reality. But instead of coming home with souvenirs, I came back with a husband – and years of emotional suffocation I never saw coming.

Yep! I married a man I'd known for just two months.

At the time, I honestly believed I was the luckiest girl alive. Here was someone who looked me in the eye and said he wanted to be with me forever. I didn't care that he didn't have a full-time job. I didn't care that he had no formal education. He was handsome, kind to me and, in just eight weeks of attention, affection and the illusion of safety, I was sold.

Why?

When you grow up in a home where love feels conditional – where silence, control and shame eat dinner with you every night – anyone who offers you a little care feels like salvation.

He wasn't rich. He wasn't driven. He wasn't emotionally stable. But you know what he was? Present. And to someone like me, that felt like everything. I wasn't looking for a soulmate. I was looking for a rescuer.

Like many women aching to feel wanted, I mistook attention for affection.

We got married quickly. No grand ceremony. No wedding dress. I didn't even tell my parents. We were just two scared souls clinging to each other, hoping that would be enough.

In the first three months, I kept telling myself it would get better. That he'd settle down. That he'd become the man I needed. But he didn't. In fact, he began to rely on me for everything – emotionally, physically and financially. We went through times where we couldn't afford to eat. We had to borrow money just to buy groceries.

Still, I convinced myself it would all be okay. I loved him. And surely my love could change him, right?

I was scared of failing. Scared of being judged. Scared of being alone again. So I stayed. For nineteen years.

We lived more like housemates than husband and wife. I told myself it was better to have someone at home than to come back to an empty house. But truthfully – I was the loneliest woman in a marriage. I wasn't just alone – I was invisible.

I tried to fix it the only way I knew how: by fixing me.

Maybe if I became more agreeable, he'd soften.

Maybe if I earned more, he'd respect me.

Maybe if I worked harder, smiled more, cleaned better … he'd love me.

But love doesn't work like that. It's not earned through over-functioning. It's not sustained through self-abandonment. And it's definitely not built on obligation or pity.

Then one day, he looked me straight in the eye and said the sentence that shattered the illusion: "You're not even worth a pile of dirt."

That was my wake-up moment.

Nineteen years of trying, hoping, proving – and that was all I meant to him? I realised then that nothing I did would ever be enough. Not because I wasn't valuable but because I was trying to make someone see my worth – and he was never capable of it.

That's when I left.

Martha's Lesson

Don't marry – or stay with – someone just because they showed up when you were bleeding. That's not love. That's emotional first aid.

He's not responsible for your happiness. He should add spice to your life, not drain the flavour out of it. Relationships are an investment and learning when to stop pouring in when you're not getting any return is how you protect your heart and honour your energy.

If someone ever says you're 'too much', smile sweetly and say, "Too much for the wrong person? Absolutely."

Straighten your crown, walk away, and know this: He wasn't the one. He was just the *Wrong Right Guy*.

Lesson 2: Business Bling and Emotional Burnout

Building an empire means nothing if you lose yourself inside it.

If you looked at my life on paper, you'd think, "Wow, she's killing it!"

International make-up artist. Multiple awards. Glowing reviews. Travelling for high-profile clients. Running a thriving *Yeah The Girls 40+* Community. Public praise. Smiles in every photo.

But behind the lashes, the lip gloss, and the success?

There are so many moments where I've become the greatest pretender. I was falling apart – overwhelmed, burned out, but too scared to tell anyone. I held it together on the outside because I was terrified of being seen as weak on the inside.

Let's get one thing straight: I never faked my talent. I earned every bit of my success with hard work, long nights and relentless passion. I *knew* I was good at what I did – I still am. I'm confident in my abilities.

But what I did fake – and very well – was how I was coping.

No-one teaches you that being 'successful' can feel so isolating. That you can be celebrated publicly and still feel completely unseen privately.

I spent endless nights replying to posts in the community, leaving heartfelt support to members. I genuinely love my girls. I've learned so much from them seeing what they go through, understanding their heartbreaks and healing. It gives me purpose. It fills my heart. It makes everything feel meaningful.

But even purpose can get heavy.

There are moments where the pressure builds. The responsibility. The conflicts. The constant expectation that I'll have the answers – that I'll always know what to do.

And that's where it gets lonely.

I thought being busy meant I was doing something right. That if I just kept pushing, kept showing up, kept serving – I'd finally feel like I belonged.

But sometimes, on those late, lonely nights, when I'm bone-tired and the to-do list never ends, I just wish I didn't have to carry so much.

I had built an incredible career. But I'd built it on top of exhaustion, people-pleasing, self-doubt and a constant fear of not being good enough. We're taught that hustle equals worth. That if we're not busy, we're lazy. That if we rest, we'll fall behind. That saying 'no' is selfish.

And women? We take it even further. We over-give. We over-deliver. We over-compensate. All just to be taken seriously.

But what happens when your calendar is full and your soul is empty? What happens when you're pouring into others while your own cup is bone dry? Eventually, you burn out. Not just physically. Emotionally. Spiritually. And burnout doesn't look like flames. It looks like numbness. It sounds like 'I'm fine' when you're anything but. It shows up as success that doesn't feel successful.

At one point, I asked myself: "If I stop doing ... who am I?" And that hit hard because I realised I didn't know. I'd tied my entire identity to what I produced, how much I helped, how often I was available. I wasn't running a business anymore – I was running myself into the ground.

So I made a decision: to put *me* back on my own list of priorities.

I started saying no – gently, firmly, without guilt. I began protecting my time because burnout isn't a badge of honour, it's a bill your body will eventually collect. I started working with intention, not desperation. And slowly, I began to remember who I was outside the expectations, outside the pressure and outside the need to constantly prove my value.

Martha's Lesson

Success isn't measured by how busy you are, it's measured by how well you know yourself while building your dream. Your business should fuel your life, not consume it.

Asking for help, taking time off, or saying "I need space" isn't weakness – it's *necessary* for your longevity. You can be ambitious without self-sacrifice. You can rest without guilt. You can have boundaries and still be brilliant.

And if the price of your success is your peace – it's too damn expensive.

Lesson 3: Healed Women Love Differently

I didn't find the one by luck — I became the woman who no longer feared love.

When I left my marriage of nineteen years, I wasn't just walking away from a man; I was walking into the unknown. And to be honest, I was scared. I had no idea what a healthy relationship even looked like. I just knew what I *never* wanted again.

And that was a start.

But here's the thing no-one tells you: healing doesn't magically make you 'ready'. It makes you *aware*. And with awareness comes responsibility.

I didn't just want love again; I wanted to understand it. I didn't want to fall back into old patterns, to mistake attention for affection or to confuse control with care. I wanted to *learn* how to do this properly. So, I made a decision: I went on over 200 dates!

At one point, I was on *eight* different dating apps, talking to five or more candidates at a time.

And yes, people laughed. Some even called me a 'professional dater', but I wore that title with pride because every single date was a lesson. A filter. A reminder of what I would – and wouldn't – allow anymore.

I wasn't dating out of desperation. I wasn't searching for validation. I simply didn't want to waste time. I was on a mission to find someone who matched the *new version* of me, not the wounded woman I used to be.

And most importantly, I wasn't afraid to walk away if it didn't feel right.

I also did over forty relationship courses. From masculine and feminine energy to trauma bonding, communication skills and understanding how men express love – I studied it all. Not to please men. Not to become the 'perfect partner'. I did them because I *genuinely* didn't understand how relationships worked – and I refused to stay in the dark just to keep repeating history.

I studied the hell out of love. I trained myself not just to *get* a relationship ... but to *keep* a healthy one. I didn't want to be led by fear anymore – fear of rejection, abandonment or being 'too much'. I wanted to be led by knowledge, by desire, and by *clarity*.

All that work gave birth to my Five-Sentence Filter – a quick, smart way to weed out time-wasters. It also led to my Five Stages of Dating, a framework to help women date with confidence and logic.

The first attraction is easy but the real skill is keeping the love alive and *growing it* for the long haul.

Then, I met Melcome.

After 200 dates and a mountain of self-work, he showed up. Not as a saviour. Not as some magical missing piece. But as a man who *matched* me – not one who mirrored my trauma.

He saw *me*. The playful, strong, soft, stubborn, open-hearted woman I had become. With him, I didn't have to chase. I didn't have to shrink. I didn't have to second-guess myself. For the first time, I understood what *peace* feels like in love.

And here's the twist – it was never really about *him*. It was about the woman I became to *attract* him. It was about how I *stopped giving up on myself*, even when the world told me I was too old, too broken, too late.

I wasn't late. I was just finally ready.

That's what healed women do. We don't wait for luck. We don't settle because we're tired. We don't let shame, time or critics stop us. We *decide* that love is worth it – and so are we.

Martha's Lesson

Healed women love differently. We don't chase, fix or beg. We *choose*, *co-create* and *communicate*.

And if you're still on the journey? Please don't give up on love just because it hasn't found you yet. Become the version of you who won't miss it when it does because when *healthy* love finally arrives, it feels like home – not a battlefield.

And no matter what the world says, you are never too old, too broken or too far gone for a second chance in love.

I'm living proof.

Lesson 4: The Two-Second Shift That Rebuilt My Life

Change doesn't take years – it takes a second of truth, followed by a second of action.

I didn't always know how to manage overwhelm. For a long time, I ran on adrenaline, duty and the fear of falling behind. But eventually, life cornered me. And I was forced to create something that saved me – and now, helps others too. I call it the 2-Second Mindset Shift and it goes like this:

The first second: awareness and acceptance

This is the moment we realise something's going on inside us. Not to fight it. Not to judge it. Just to *notice* and *accept*: I'm not okay right now. I feel defensive. I'm spiralling again.

This awareness is where all change begins. Without it, we stay stuck in the same loop – repeating patterns, hoping for different results, getting more frustrated each time. But once we become aware, and *accept* what we're feeling, that's when we stop fighting ourselves. We start listening and in that moment of clarity – we unlock choice.

The second second: action with intention

This isn't just about doing something for the sake of doing it. It's about taking action that's fuelled by *why*.

Let's face it – if motivation were enough, we'd all be millionaires on kale diets. But human willpower is short-lived and that's why so many people start something and give up when it gets uncomfortable.

The only thing that keeps us going is the *reason* behind the action. The purpose. The desire. The 'I'm doing this because it matters'. That's what turns a small step into a powerful shift.

So, how did I find my confidence in a crisis?

I was a multi-award-winning make-up artist. That was my world. But then Covid hit and the world shut down. With weddings cancelled and events gone, I was forced to sit with myself and that's when it happened – the *first second*.

I realised I'd spent over twenty years helping women look confident on the outside. But deep down, many were still hiding behind their lashes and lipstick. I saw myself in them and I *accepted* that I had more to offer than just beauty.

In the *second second*, I took action. I created *Super Confidence Coaching* – a business built to help women eliminate insecurity not just from the outside, but from the inside, too. I never imagined I'd become a confidence coach but it turns out that the same skills I used in the beauty chair translated into transformation.

That two-second shift is what helped me rebuild my career and find my purpose.

And, how did I grow an empire from grief?

When I started building *Yeah The Girls 40 Plus*, I was grieving and depressed, but something inside me told me – this matters. I saw the loneliness. The silence. The struggles women over 40 were carrying behind the scenes. I told people, "I'm building an empire." They laughed. I saw the eye-rolls. The polite nods.

It stung.

But instead of shrinking, I used the two-second shift again. I acknowledged my embarrassment. And I took action *anyway*.

Why? Because I had a *why* that mattered more than their doubt.

Now, that little spark has become a national movement. Thousands of women have found their voice, their joy, their confidence again because I didn't give up in those two seconds of discomfort.

Martha's Lesson

Overwhelm doesn't mean stop – it means *shift*.

Take one second to get honest. Take one second to move with purpose. That's how you build empires. That's how you build *yourself*. Not in giant leaps but in tiny moments of clarity and courage – one second at a time.

Final lesson: Do Not Follow What Martha Did and You Will Be Very Successful

I made every mistake so you don't have to.

If you've made it this far, you've probably laughed, maybe cried and definitely said, "Wait, she did what?!"

Yes. I married the wrong man after two months. I stayed in a loveless marriage for nineteen years. I burned myself out in business trying to prove I was worthy. I went on over 200 dates while being called a 'professional dater'. I built a community while grieving and doubting myself.

So why on earth would I name this chapter – and this entire message – do not follow what Martha did and you will be very successful?

I don't want you to follow my mistakes; I want you to learn from them.

With everything I've experienced in life, it would be understandable if I turned to darkness. But I didn't because I don't want another woman to suffer in silence the way I once did. I don't want anyone else to feel like they have no options left.

My life has been colourful – not always joyful, but always alive. And in the face of deep pain, I chose to become the light. I chose to be hope. I chose to be the reminder that it's never too late to begin again.

Take the time you need to breathe, regroup and come back stronger. Set a return date if you must. Just promise me this: never keep going on an empty cup. Running on fumes is not bravery. It's slow self-erasure.

What I Want You to Remember From Each Lesson

Don't marry someone because you're afraid of being alone.

My first lesson, The Wrong Right Guy, taught me that love built on fear is not love. Don't wait nineteen years to realise your worth. Don't shrink yourself just to have someone beside you.

Don't burn yourself to keep your dreams alive.

My second lesson, Business Bling & Burnout, showed me that success without self-care is just slow self-destruction. Don't confuse busyness with purpose.

Don't give up on love – but don't let it define you either.

My third lesson, Healed Women Love Differently, proved that second chances come when we stop settling. Study love. Learn yourself. Date with dignity, not desperation.

Don't wait for the perfect moment to change — take two seconds.

My fourth lesson, The Two-Second Mindset Shift, gave me the tools I now live and breathe. First, awareness. Then, intentional action. No more waiting for permission. No more fighting the same battle with the same broken sword.

And finally – don't stay quiet.

My fifth and final lesson, The Power of One Voice, reminded me that what once made me ashamed has now become my legacy. The most powerful thing I've ever done was to speak up.

So, don't follow what I did. Don't let life happen to you. Make choices that are led by love, not fear. By awareness, not autopilot. By desire, not desperation.

But also – don't be afraid to fall like I did. Don't be ashamed to rebuild. And never, ever be embarrassed by how long it took you to come home to yourself because here's the truth: I had to be the girl who got it all wrong to become the woman who helps others get it right.

My Hope For You

I don't want you to become another Martha. I want you to become *you*. Braver. Bolder. Louder. Wiser.

And if sharing my messy, unfiltered, very human journey helps even one woman stop suffering in silence then I've done my job.

Success isn't about a perfect timeline. It's about learning who you are, and living that, unapologetically.

So, no, don't follow what Martha did.

But absolutely follow what she learned.

You will be very successful.

Martha Mok *is the Director of the* Yeah The Girls 40 Plus *community, a confidence coach, international speaker and the proud owner of a life full of 'what not to do' lessons. She helps women over forty rebuild their confidence, rediscover self-worth and finally stop wasting time on the 'Wrong Right Guy'.*

After surviving bullying, abuse and heartbreak, Martha turned her pain into purpose and grew a community of over 35,000 women. Along the way, she created platforms like the Celebrate Women Awards *and* Celebrating Women Expo *so women could be seen, heard and celebrated.*

When Martha is not leading, coaching or speaking, she's usually enjoying good food, losing herself in a movie or working on her karaoke game. Life isn't about being perfect – it's about owning your story and singing it out loud.

And Now, A Toast

JJ Collins

Can we please just take a moment
    For all the ladies in our lives,
The ones who dare and dream and wish
The ones who manage to survive.

There is no guidebook for this life
Our one and only chance,
And our existence on this earth
Is so fleeting ...
Gone, in just a glance.

With all the grace and courage
We fumble on and on
Trying hard to please the others
Far out, it just won't stop!

Despite the hardships and frustrations
We find the gemstones and the treasure
Using their illustrious shimmer
That we can see, right there,
Inside, you and me!

So, raise your glass now,
Way up high
Be it bubbles, brew or tea,
And say a cheer for those you know
Who've shown you something,
You simply couldn't see.
Cheers, Salud, Prost and Kanpai, Skal, Cin Cin and Gan Bay.

www.ingramcontent.com/pod-product-compliance
Lightning Source LLC
Chambersburg PA
CBHW060350080526
44583CB00012B/252